DUTCH SCHULTZ

DUTCH SCHULTZ

The Brazen Beer Baron
of New York

GANGSTER

by Nate Hendley

PUBLISHED BY ALTITUDE PUBLISHING LTD.
1500 Railway Avenue, Canmore, Alberta T1W 1P6
www.altitudepublishing.com
1-800-957-6888

Extreme care has been taken to ensure that all information presented in
this book is accurate and up to date. Neither the author nor the
publisher can be held responsible for any errors.

Publisher	Stephen Hutchings
Associate Publisher	Kara Turner
Series Editor	Jill Foran
Editor	Pat Kozak
Digital Photo Colouring	Bryan Pezzi

We acknowledge the financial support of the Government
of Canada through the Book Publishing Industry Development
Program (BPIDP) for our publishing activities.

Altitude GreenTree Program
Altitude Publishing will plant twice as many trees as were used
in the manufacturing of this product.

Cataloging in Publication Data

Hendley, Nate
Dutch Schultz / Nate Hendley.

(Amazing stories)
Includes bibliographical references.
ISBN 1-55265-104-5

1. Schultz, Dutch, 1900 or 1-1935. 2. Criminals--New York
(State)--New York--Biography.
3. Racketeering--New York (State)--New York--History--20th century. I.
Title. II. Series: Amazing
stories (Canmore, Alta.)

HV6248.S39H45 2005   364.1'092
C2005-902433-X

An application for the trademark for Amazing Stories™
has been made and the registered trademark is pending.

Printed and bound in Canada by Friesens
2 4 6 8 9 7 5 3 1

The history of organized crime in New York City has long been glamorized through
books, magazines, film, and television. Inevitably, anyone researching this history
will be presented with many different "true accounts" of underworld events. In
regards to each title in the Amazing Stories series, Altitude Publishing has left it
up to the author to choose which version of events he or she wishes to convey.

This book is dedicated to Cheryl Melkert,
who tried her best.

Contents

Prologue 11

Chapter 1 A Criminal Star is Born 12

Chapter 2 Prohibition Blues 27

Chapter 3 Bullet Ballet 39

Chapter 4 The Long Arm of The Dutchman 54

Chapter 5 Lucky Numbers. 63

Chapter 6 Public Enemy Number One 79

Chapter 7 A Taxing Experience. 91

Chapter 8 Dewey v. the Dutchman 106

Chapter 9 The Chop House Massacre. 118

Chapter 10 The Fading Star. 127

Epilogue 134

Further Reading 136

Prologue

October 24, 1935

The Dutchman was dying. The bullet in his gut had caused massive internal injuries and sent his temperature soaring. Staring fixedly at the ceiling from his hospital bed, Arthur Flegenheimer — aka Dutch Schultz — cried and babbled. In his delirium, he began weaving a weird tapestry of unconnected phrases, names, and oaths.

A police stenographer sat by the gangster's side, taking down every word. The authorities hoped Schultz might reveal Mob secrets in his final monologue. But Dutch proved as elusive in his dying hours as he had been in life.

"No, no. There are only 10 of us and there are 10 million fighting somewhere in front of you, so get your onions up and we will throw up the truce flag," he raved. "Oh, please let me up. Please shift me. Police are here. Communistic ... strike ... baloney ... honestly, this is a habit I get; sometimes I give it and sometimes I don't. Oh, I am all in. That settles it. Are you sure? Please let me get in and eat. Let him harass himself to you and then bother you."

None of it made any sense to the police. They kept listening, however, as Schultz rambled on, his mind journeying back and forth over the course of his brief, but spectacular, criminal life.

Chapter 1
A Criminal
Star is Born

rthur Flegenheimer was born in the Manhattan working-class neighborhood of Yorkville on August 6, 1902. His mother and father were German Jews who had fled Europe to seek a better life in America. What Emma and Herman Flegenheimer found instead were crowded tenements and grinding poverty.

When Arthur was very young, his parents moved out of Yorkville and into the South Bronx. There, they raised their son and young daughter, Helen, in the tough Bergen and Webster Avenue neighborhood. Life in the Bronx, to put it charitably, was awful.

At the turn of the 20th century, 3.4 million people lived in New York City — most of them poor. Destitute New

Yorkers had to deal with lousy housing, rampant pollution, unhealthy food and water, horrid workplaces, and vicious crime. Criminals worked the buildings, banks, and offices, and youth gangs roamed the streets. The latter were every bit as vicious and predatory as the street gangs of today.

Police did what they could, but they were outnumbered and often outgunned by the crooks. Besides, many cops and their political bosses were in the pay of local crime lords. On a municipal level, New York was still controlled by Tammany Hall, the colloquial name of the local corrupt Democratic political machine. Established shortly after the American Revolution as a patriotic social club, Tammany Hall quickly grew into a political force to be reckoned with. By the time the Flegenheimers set foot in New York, Tammany Hall was the dominant power in municipal politics. Tammany "bosses" controlled city contracts and patronage and luxuriated in graft. It was whispered that Tammany officials could literally get away with murder. These rumors might not have been true, but they gave an indication of the fantastic levels of corruption in the Big Apple.

Emma and Herman tried to do right by their children, or at least Emma did. When Arthur was old enough, they enrolled him in Public School 12. Arthur proved to be a reasonably intelligent, if not diligent, student. While Arthur later stated that he enjoyed his classes, the majority of his education came from outside the schoolroom. Then, as now, New York City teemed with young children who sought relief from their bleak homes and poor families by taking to the streets. Arthur was no exception. By his early teens, he was already part of a youth gang that hung around Bergen Street, smoking, thieving, shooting pool, and causing trouble.

When Arthur was 14, Herman Flegenheimer abandoned his family, forever embittering his son. With the main breadwinner in the household gone, Emma took whatever jobs she could find in order to feed her children. She worked as a janitor in a slum tenement and took in washing to earn some extra cash.

Arthur used his father's disappearance as an excuse to stop going to school. In later years, he claimed he dropped out to help his mother support the family. He worked briefly as a roofer, sold subway transfers on the street, and toiled in a print shop as a feeder and pressman.

Young Arthur didn't care much for these subsistence gigs. He had his eye on more lucrative, if illicit, ways of earning his keep. He began hanging around a club that served as a haunt for area residents and local gangsters, hoping the hoods would offer some useful career guidance.

Sure enough, a neighborhood mobster named Marcel Poffo took an interest in him. Poffo had a criminal record and a bad reputation, which greatly impressed the wide-eyed teen. Even though Poffo was only one year older than Arthur, he acted as a substitute father for the aspiring delinquent. Poffo began to mentor Arthur in the ways and means of the underworld. Arthur was starstruck by the low-level gangster; Poffo's fearless, "don't-give-a-damn" attitude was a stark contrast to the broken spirit of most of the men in the neighborhood. When Arthur compared Poffo's bulging wallet to the empty pockets of other Bergen Street males, it seemed further evidence of the futility of taking legitimate work.

To his mother's dismay, Arthur launched his own crime wave. With the help of his Bergen Street comrades, the fledgling crook stole packages from delivery vehicles, shoplifted from neighborhood stores, and broke into homes. Local gamblers who hadn't paid "protection" money to Poffo suddenly found their games interrupted by the arrival of Arthur and his cohorts, demanding tribute as the price for avoiding personal injury. Mrs. Flegenheimer's son was gaining a reputation as a local tough-guy, someone the neighborhood cops kept their eye on.

Arthur proved fearless in his criminal endeavors. Poffo was pleased. His little protégé was learning fast. Not fast enough, however, to avoid a jail sentence.

On December 12, 1919, Arthur was arrested for burglarizing a Bronx apartment. Some accounts say he was caught in the act, burglar tools in hand. To the authorities, Arthur identified himself as "Charles Harmon." He was sent to Blackwell's Island Penitentiary, a dismal, gray stone institution located in the middle of the East River. He was 17 years old.

Arthur proved to be less than a model prisoner. He acted up and was so unruly that he managed to get transferred to a tougher facility, Westhampton Prison Farms. But the rebellious teen didn't care much for the place and managed to escape. Arthur's dash for freedom didn't last long. Within 24 hours, he was recaptured and sent back to Westhampton. His jailers added two months to his sentence as punishment for leaving without permission. As the young con brooded and moped at Westhampton, enormous social changes were going on in the outside world.

In 1919, the United States Congress passed the Volstead Act. This foolish piece of legislation attempted to stamp out "Demon Rum" by federal fiat. The act made it illegal to "manufacture, sell, barter, transport, import, export, deliver, furnish or possess any intoxicating liquor," including beer and wine. The law came into effect at the stroke of midnight, January 17, 1920. Prohibition had begun, and it was the government's greatest gift to the criminal world.

Of course, the well-intentioned people who supported Prohibition didn't quite see it that way. Alcohol prohibition had come about as a result of decades of lobbying from churches and women's groups that believed booze was the bane of working-class families, and cultural conservatives who detested beer-and-wine-loving immigrants. So-called "dry" advocates believed that banning alcohol would bring America into a new world of godliness.

The spirit of the times was reflected by the over-the-top antics of the appropriately named Billy Sunday, a famous fundamentalist preacher. "The reign of tears is over," shouted Sunday at a rally in Norfolk, Virginia, after Volstead was made law. "The slums will soon be only a memory. We will turn our prisons into factories and our jails into storehouses and corncribs. Men will walk upright now, women will smile and children will laugh. Hell will be forever for rent."

Things didn't turn out quite the way Sunday hoped. From the moment the Volstead Act went into effect, it was widely ignored. The urge to drink proved stronger than the will to obey the law. Almost overnight, an enormous black market in booze sprang up, serviced by young, enterprising criminals.

These aspiring mobsters brought in booze from Canada, where it remained legal for distilleries to produce liquor, or they made it themselves in bathtubs and secret stills. Quality control was nonexistent; some bootleg booze was spiked with industrial alcohol and other poisons. Instead of getting imbibers drunk, the stuff would make them very ill, or even kill them.

Against this backdrop of social engineering, Arthur was released from Westhampton. He returned home, in 1921, to the cheers of his neighborhood street gang. The Bergen Street crew was delighted to see him back. They viewed doing time as a rite of passage, much in the same way that other teens might view the Boy Scouts or a stint in the army.

Arthur had entered the pen as a mere boy. Now, after serving 15 months, he had hardened into manhood. Besides toughening him up, the sentence offered Arthur the kind of career guidance he might have otherwise lacked. Far from "reforming" him, his time in the slammer made him more determined than ever to stick with the criminal life. Living on the wrong side of the law seemed far more profitable — not to mention fun — than taking a legitimate job, despite the threat of incarceration.

As a young hood, Arthur wasn't much to look at — and he didn't try to improve on nature. He had black hair, which was usually dirty and combed to one side, a scowl of a mouth, and coarse, puffy features. A chorus girl would later describe him as looking like "Bing Crosby with his face bashed in."

At age 19, the stockily built Arthur stood roughly 5 feet 7 inches tall. Although he wasn't physically impressive, he was fearless and had the air of a man destined for greater things. Arthur had survived jail with his criminal spirit intact, and because of this, his fellow gang members felt he deserved a new name. Arthur Flegenheimer just wouldn't cut it. He needed a handle with more zip.

Someone in the Bergen Street crew remembered an old-time criminal called "Dutch Schultz." This individual had been a member of the notorious Frog Hollow Gang in the Bronx. The Frog Hollows had specialized in "white slavery" — another term for prostitution. The police had crushed the gang some time before World War I. The Bergen Street crew was pretty sure the original Dutch Schultz wouldn't mind if they appropriated his alias. The guy was probably dead or in prison, anyway.

Arthur didn't have any objections to being renamed

"Dutch," even though he was of German descent. It was a common tag in those days for anyone from central Europe. In any case, Schultz was a better moniker for a young, aspiring criminal than Flegenheimer.

Armed with a new name and appropriate credentials, Dutch Schultz — or the Dutchman, as he was often called — set out to make his mark on the underworld. He soon found himself a job as a driver for Arnold Rothstein, a well-known gangster. Like Schultz, Rothstein hailed from a Jewish family. Unlike Schultz, Rothstein was extremely rich and powerful — possibly the biggest gangster in pre-Prohibition America.

A charmer with good manners, Rothstein had made an illicit fortune through gambling and bookmaking. He later branched out into venture financing, and provided seed money to aspiring gangsters with innovative criminal schemes. Nicknamed "the Brain" by the media, Rothstein served as the inspiration for the fictitious mobster villain Meyer Wolfshiem in F. Scott Fitzgerald's classic novel, *The Great Gatsby*. It was rumored that Rothstein had "fixed" the 1919 World Series. In fact, he hadn't. But the rumor stuck because Rothstein seemed powerful enough to pull off such a scam.

While Rothstein had a reputation for grace, money, and pizzazz, Schultz's initial duties for his new boss were anything but glamorous. With Prohibition in full swing, Rothstein became a key supplier of illicit liquor in New York City. Schultz was one of many small cogs in Rothstein's booze distribution setup, but he was ambitious and told himself the job would lead to bigger and better things. Schultz spent his time driving trucks filled with bootleg booze to the countless speakeasies that had sprung up in the city. By 1922, there were around 5000 speakeasies operating in the Big Apple, slaking the thirst of alcohol-parched New Yorkers.

During this formative phase of his life, Schultz kept his eyes and options open and paid close attention to how the criminal bosses around him went about their business. He also rubbed shoulders with other entry-level employees in the bootleg business. One worker stood out — a dark-haired thug named Charles Luciano. Luciano, whose real name was Salvatore Lucania, was born in 1897 in Sicily. His parents had fled the Old World for the land of liberty, freedom, and economic opportunity, just as the Flegenheimers had.

Luciano had also grown up in a tough New York neighborhood and turned to crime at an early age. At 10 years old, he was arrested for shoplifting. This arrest didn't deter the lad from pursuing his intended career. By his teens, he was running a protection racket with his pals. The racket worked like this: Luciano and Co. would threaten people with a beating unless they forked over "protection" money.

In 1915, Luciano went to reform school for peddling morphine and heroin. He was something of a pioneer in this field, being that the federal government had outlawed dope only the year before.

Like Schultz, Luciano was hungry and ambitious. They were both determined to rise above the world of petty crime and make names for themselves. However, neither of them had any idea of how famous — or infamous — they would become. Despite their similar backgrounds, they were wary of each other and never became pals. Schultz preferred to keep his own counsel, in any case.

During the 1920s, when they were both rising in the underworld ranks, the young men became part of the Jack "Legs" Diamond gang. Diamond was one of the local big shots in crime — considerably more powerful than Schultz's first mentor, Marcel Poffo. The story was that Legs got the nickname from his ability to outrun the police during a misspent youth. Luciano was also to pick up a nickname during his career — Lucky. According to underworld legend, he acquired the moniker after surviving a kidnap and torture session at the hands of enemies.

In 1925, Schultz briefly became a deputy sheriff in the Bronx. This was an unpaid position, but it allowed him to carry a gun — a useful benefit in his line of work. Schultz won the appointment from Edward Flynn, a Democratic Party leader in the Bronx who was rumored to be friendly to the Mob. Flynn would later claim he made hundreds of appointments a year and had no idea Schultz was a criminal.

It didn't matter much anyway. After being picked up in a police raid on Legs Diamond's club in 1926, Schultz's deputy badge was revoked.

The chummy relationship between crooks and politicians was carefully nurtured by both sides. The mayor of New

York City, elected the same year Schultz lost his deputy badge, was a colorful showman named Jimmy Walker. Walker didn't exactly strain himself to capture gangsters. Throughout his corrupt reign, he had many close and curious relationships with underworld figures and turned a blind eye to the trade in bootleg booze.

New York practically floated on liquor. The number of illegal drinking spots expanded to astonishing proportions throughout the 1920s. According to some sources, there were as many as 30,000 speakeasies in the city by 1927.

Schultz continued to benefit from the freewheeling ways of his fellow New Yorkers. His flexibility and willingness to pick up new skills put him in good stead with his criminal comrades. He graduated from driving booze trucks to working in a Bronx speakeasy. The establishment was called the Hub Social Club and was run by Joey Noe, one of Schultz's buddies. Hidden away in a tenement building, it wasn't the classiest place in the world — but it was a start.

As a bartender in an illicit drinking establishment, Schultz often had to step in to settle violent disputes between customers or rival criminals. The slum-like ambience of the Hub Social Club lent itself to less-than-genteel behavior among its clientele. The low-life patrons were quick to anger and hard to reason with. And the lousy rotgut served up by Noe didn't improve their moods any. One sly glance or a mildly insulting word was enough to set them off into a flurry of alcohol-sodden fisticuffs.

If later tales are to be believed, Schultz was quick to respond to such outbreaks of ungentlemanly behavior. While not hugely muscular, Schultz was tough. He would apparently leap right in when his clients started mixing it up and bring chaos to order with his fists and curses. Some accounts state that a wooden baseball bat played a prominent role in Schultz's bartender/bouncer duties.

The Dutchman soon gained a reputation for his violence and ferocious temper — attributes that earned him respect and helped him climb the underworld ladder quickly. He had not been on the bottom rungs of the bootleg business for long when he got his big break.

In 1928, when he was in his mid-20s, he made the leap from bartender to businessman. Noe, who suggested forming a business partnership, made this career advancement possible. Noe was only slightly taller than Schultz but considerably more formidable. He was one of very few people who could get away with barking orders at Schultz. He was also allowed to call Schultz "Arthur" — a privilege the Dutchman granted to only a select few. In return, Noe allowed his friend to dream big and think of a life beyond petty hustling and minor thievery. If Poffo helped Schultz get his foot in the underworld door, Noe pushed him to a whole new level of gangster activity.

Schultz and Noe opened up a chain of speakeasies around the Bronx. They also started peddling beer to other speakeasy owners. Schultz and Noe bought their suds from an illicit brewer named Frankie Dunn, whose operations were based in Union City, New Jersey. Most of their customers were Irish saloon owners who had refused to throw in the towel with the advent of Prohibition. Instead, these barkeeps had opened up new underground drinking establishments. Because these bars operated illegally, they were vulnerable to the outreach efforts of criminals such as the Dutchman and Noe. The Better Business Bureau didn't register complaints from the black market.

Like any good entrepreneurs, Schultz and Noe plowed their profits back into their company. They purchased their own trucks, which they guarded with their lives. They took turns riding "shotgun," in much the same way as drivers used to guard stagecoaches in the Old West. Schultz spent many hours sitting in the passenger seat armed with a gun to deter rival gangsters from hijacking them. The slick partners soon opened more speakeasies around town and rapidly expanded their business.

As up-and-coming businessmen, Schultz and Noe developed some highly effective marketing techniques. The pair confronted speakeasy owners and threatened to beat them senseless if they didn't accept their beer. The threat alone was usually enough to convince the owners to join Schultz and Noe's rapidly expanding customer base. Certainly, no one signed up because they liked the duo's product — Schultz and Noe's beer was generally awful, diluted as much as possible for maximum profitability.

Occasionally, the business partners ran into some resistance. Joe Rock, for example, proved to be as tough as his last name. Along with his brother, John, Joe was in the bootlegging business. The Rock brothers were Irish, which, according to national stereotype, meant they were very stubborn. In spite of his heritage, John Rock proved to be a most amenable client. When Schultz and Noe came calling, John quickly agreed to withdraw his services from the booze market. Joe, on the other hand, was mule-headed. He refused to be intimidated by the duo, which was a bad mistake.

Faced with a problem like Joe, Schultz and Noe decided that they needed to set an example. They arranged for Joe to be kidnapped and taken to a desolate locale in the city. There, they ordered their thugs to hang Joe by his thumbs from a meat hook and beat him viciously. And that wasn't even the worst of it. Out of sheer sadistic spite, their men wrapped a gauze bandage over Joe's eyes. This bandage had been liberally coated with discharge from a gonorrhea sore.

It's unclear if Schultz enjoyed having Joe tortured or just considered it good business practice. In either case, the one-time petty thief from Bergen Street was serious about teaching the Irish bootlegger a lesson. By the time Schultz and Noe's crew was done with him, the stubborn Mr. Rock was unfit for bar duty.

Joe Rock's parents arranged to cough up $35,000 for the release of their stubborn son. After they paid his ransom, Joe was released into their tender care. Unfortunately, he soon went blind from the vicious treatment meted out to him.

Through such acts of thuggery, Schultz's criminal star began to rise rapidly in the Bronx. A good student of underworld behavior, Schultz had learned a particularly valuable lesson from his mobster mentors: might made right. In the criminal jungle, it was shoot or be shot, torture or be tortured. It was survival of the sleaziest, a Darwinian competition that rewarded the most violent urban savages.

If Schultz was bothered by the reality of this world, he didn't let on. A happy entrepreneur, he expanded his fleet of beer trucks and looked forward to joining the mobster major leagues with his pal Noe.

Chapter 2
Prohibition Blues

As their business expanded, Schultz and Noe took care to hire talented employees. They soon had a pack of tough guys working for — and protecting — them. Most of these helpers were Jewish or Irish.

The ring of steel around Schultz and Noe included newcomers such as Abe "Bo" Weinberg, a hulking two-fisted brute; Abe's slightly more refined brother, George; Larry Carney; Joey Rao; and Edward "Fats" McCarthy. But many of the other "soldiers" in the group were childhood friends of Schultz's or Noe's, including Thomas "Fatty" Walsh and the handsome, arrogant Vincent Coll.

Tall, blond, and baby-faced, Coll had been part of the gang that had hung out with Schultz back on Bergen

Street. His angelic good looks belied his vicious temper and emotional instability. Bullet tough, Coll was dangerously unstable — even by gangster standards — and fearless to the point of suicidal recklessness. His brother, Peter, was part of the Schultz/Noe crew as well, although he wasn't one to make waves.

With such an impressive employee roster, it was no surprise that Schultz and Noe's business expanded at a phenomenal pace throughout 1928. The Dutchman and his partner began buying beer from other illicit brewers to meet growing demand. Their new suppliers included Owen Madden, a British-born mobster who had been involved in New York rackets since World War 1. Known as "Owney the Killer," Madden was a big name in crime circles. That he was willing to work with Schultz and Noe was an indication of their growing stature in the booze trade.

From their extremely modest beginnings in the Bronx, Schultz and Noe found themselves dealing beer all over Manhattan, in neighborhoods such as Washington Heights and Harlem. Their success had more to do with brutal marketing methods than brainpower. It didn't take a business genius to make money out of Prohibition. All you needed were guts, guns, and a total lack of conscience or remorse.

Schultz and Noe bought more trucks and expanded their product line to include hard liquor and other alcoholic beverages. They also established elaborate loading facilities to prevent their booze from being stolen.

One such facility was called "the Tins." Located near the Mott Haven railway yards, the Tins had a handy system of industrial-strength elevators. Empty trucks were driven in and magically transported to a hidden loading area. The vehicles would be packed with crates of beer and were then sent on their way.

Schultz and Noe also established a nifty new headquarters for themselves. They moved their HQ from the Bronx to East 149th Street in Manhattan. Among other decorative touches, the new command center had steel-lined office walls and a bulletproof front door. It was the perfect decor for cutting-edge criminals. Anyone who wanted to enter the facility was given the once-over by a guard standing behind a peephole. More guards, toting rifles and other weapons, kept the peace inside the building.

Schultz and Noe had good reason to be cautious. By setting up shop in Manhattan, they were encroaching on the turf of Legs Diamond, Schultz's former gang boss. Diamond was not pleased to see rival gangsters selling bootleg booze in his own backyard.

For all the animosity building between the two men, Diamond didn't raid Schultz's headquarters. He probably considered such a move to be foolhardy. Besides, there were other ways to put the upstarts out of business. The police, however, took the direct approach. At one point, they sacked the Schultz/Noe command center, seizing shotguns, pistols, and thousands of rounds of ammunition in the process.

Schultz and Noe weren't afraid of Legs Diamond, or the local constabulary. Not only were they back in business soon after the police raid, but they also began expanding their operations. Denizens of New York were already calling Schultz the "Beer Baron of the Bronx."

Despite his success and new position of power, Schultz continued to dress more like a pauper than a baron. Unlike other mobsters, who took pride in their sartorial grace, Schultz spent little money on jazzing up his image. In fact, he was miserly to the point of wearing old, dirty clothes and cheap suits. He was proud of his economy, figuring he was smarter than his clothes-conscious cohorts. Maturity and great wealth didn't change this attitude. Years later, he told reporters at one of his high-profile trials, "You take silk shirts now; I think only queers wear silk shirts. I never bought one in my life. Only a sucker will pay $15 or $20 for a silk shirt."

However, it seems Schultz was not too macho to wear silk shirts — and pricey ties — if someone else bought them. Supplicants and friends occasionally slipped him high-end threads, which Schultz eagerly donned under his cheapo suits.

He didn't go in for expensive trims and fancy hairstyles, either. Instead, the Dutchman wore his locks in a greasy side-part that made him look like a conniving file clerk. Other gangsters were appalled by his sloppy attire and took Schultz's ultra-causal appearance as evidence of his eccentricity. In one of his few concessions to fashion, Schultz usually wore a smart gray fedora. This hat became something of a trademark for him.

Even though he was a tightwad when it came to personal grooming, Schultz had a taste for the high life and enjoyed a good night on the town. He especially enjoyed clubbing with Noe, his only real friend.

The partners were finishing up one such night of carousing around dawn on October 15, 1928. They were at a gangster hangout in Harlem called the Swanee Club. This establishment featured live music, chorus girls, and a congenial atmosphere for wealthy blacks and whites. Gangsters considered the Swanee to be neutral turf — not a place to settle beefs. If rival mobsters met on the premises, club etiquette dictated that one of them would leave.

When the two brew kings finally left the club, they went their separate ways. Schultz went to work, but Noe had other ideas. Still feeling that the night — or morning — was young, he found his way to the Chateau Madrid, a nightclub on West 54th Street. As Noe was standing at the entrance to the club at around 7 a.m., a blue Cadillac pulled up alongside him. Before Noe had a chance to dive for cover, a gunman opened fire. The rounds cut through Noe's chest in spite of the bulletproof vest he wore underneath his tasteful duds. Within seconds, the barrage of bullets had struck him down. Noe sprawled on the sidewalk, bleeding from his wounds.

Thinking he had dispatched his rival, the gunman hit the gas and took off. But Noe was alive — though barely

— and had the strength to retrieve his pistol. He aimed the weapon at the rapidly departing car and squeezed off several shots. Amazingly, some of his bullets hit the gunman.

Witnesses saw the Cadillac swerve and smack into a parked car, losing a door in the process. The damaged vehicle drove off and was soon out of sight. Police found it an hour later. Inside was the lifeless body of a Legs Diamond gang member called Louis Weinberg (no relation to Bo or George). After an investigation, the police decided Weinberg was the gunman who had shot Noe, but they weren't sure if he had acted alone or as part of a team. Old Louis certainly wasn't in a position to offer any insight on the matter.

Back at the Chateau Madrid, Noe was near death. The bullets had torn him up badly. A crowd of gawkers gathered around him, horrified yet fascinated at the sight. An ambulance eventually arrived and Noe received first-aid. After patching up his wounds as best they could, the ambulance attendants took him to Roosevelt Hospital.

Tough guy that he was, Noe refused to give the police any clues as to who shot him. He mumbled something about being clipped while trying to park his car, but was otherwise silent. His reticence wasn't just gangster bravado; he knew he could be charged for murdering Louis Weinberg. Under the circumstances, it was best to say nothing.

The cops believed that Legs Diamond was behind Noe's shooting. They theorized that Diamond had arranged the Chateau Madrid ambush in the hopes of killing Schultz and Noe at the same time. The Dutchman had had a lucky escape.

Noe wasn't the only New York mobster to take a bullet that fall. Weeks after Noe's shooting, on November 4, Arnold Rothstein — the first gangster Schultz had ever worked for — was shot in the Park Central Hotel. When police found him, the Brain was lying on the floor in the hotel lobby. He had taken a bullet in the guts. Badly wounded, but still breathing, Rothstein was moved to a nearby hospital. The moneyman of the underworld refused to tell police who his assailant was or why the man might want him dead. Two days after being shot, Rothstein expired.

After sorting through a tangled web of theories, underworld gossips settled on one suspect — George McManus — and two motives. It was said that McManus murdered Rothstein over a gambling debt. This was a plausible theory, but there was another explanation. Rumor had it that Schultz had hired McManus to kill Rothstein because he was a friend of Legs Diamond — the man who had ordered Noe's murder.

According to some sources, one of Schultz's associates picked up McManus after the shooting and drove him to safety. If this was the case, then Rothstein's murder was intended to send a clear message to Legs: don't mess with the Dutchman.

Rothstein's demise might have lifted Schultz's spirits, but it did nothing to save his friend's life. Noe began wasting away. The cocky young gangster turned into a 100-pound skeletal wreck. He died on November 21, 1928.

Schultz was genuinely upset by the death of his one true friend. If it weren't for Noe, Schultz might still have been a street-corner punk, shoplifting from stores and breaking into apartments. Although he made tactical alliances with other mobsters, Schultz didn't look for a new partner once Noe was gone. He had trusted Noe with his life, but was wary of the rest of his peers. Also, there was something flattering about being the sole boss of a criminal enterprise. Schultz operated as a lone wolf, making all the big decisions himself.

One of these decisions involved his outfit's product line. Schultz stuck with bootlegging alcohol, even though other crooks were branching out into prostitution, gambling, and narcotics. At this stage, he was content to focus on one core business. Though he was by no means an underworld mastermind, he managed to ensure the loyalty of the men around him — probably because he paid them well.

Indeed, even as a solo act Schultz continued to rise in the gangster milieu. Other gangsters, including his old acquaintance Charles Luciano, were taking note of the Dutchman's success. Luciano had also attained a high rank in the criminal hierarchy, thanks to his own ruthless manner and profitable bootlegging operations.

In May 1929, Schultz took part in an epochal mob meeting on the East Coast. Dubbed the Atlantic City Conference, the event was attended by dozens of Italian, Jewish, and Irish gangsters from around the country. The multicultural gathering was unusual, for this was a time when ethnic groups tended to cleave to their own kind.

Schultz attended the meeting as part of a contingent of New York gangsters led by Luciano. The Big Apple crew also featured Frank Costello, Johnny Torrio, and Meyer Lansky. Another rising star, Lansky was unusual in that he relied on brains, not brawn, to secure his illicit profits.

The other big gang at the conference came from Chicago and included heavy hitters such as Frank Nitti and Al "Scarface" Capone. Capone was already a legend, having arranged the deaths of several members of the "Bugs" Moran gang a few months earlier. The latter were rubbed out in a bloodbath known as the St. Valentine's Day Massacre.

The conference had been organized, in part, to discuss Capone's propensity for high-profile violence. The mobsters didn't really care how many people Scarface Al killed; what worried them was the amount of publicity these murders churned up.

Like boardroom executives, the Mob tried to lay down rules that would govern their behavior and guide their careers. Instead of talking about profit margins and investment strategies, the conference-goers discussed murder and mayhem. They attempted to establish a protocol for the assassination of fellow gangsters. Under the new guidelines, a "boss" could only be whacked if other gang leaders agreed.

The conference was also notable for the absence of two

top New York gangsters: Salvatore Maranzano and Giuseppe "Joe the Boss" Masseria. Both men were probably too busy to attend, locked as they were in a bitter rivalry for the title of *capo di tutti capi* — boss of all bosses.

Maranzano had arrived in America in 1927, sent by Sicilian crime boss Don Vito Cascio Ferro to oversee the latter's interests in America. A strong admirer of one of history's greatest figures, Julius Caesar, Maranzano wanted to bring order, discipline, and structure to New York City's disparate gangs. His goal was to make crime thoroughly organized, with clearly demarcated territories, responsibilities, and chains of command. At the top, of course, would be Maranzano himself, presiding over New York like a modern-day Caesar.

Naturally, Masseria wasn't eager to let this happen. Masseria was also Sicilian-born but had been living in the U.S. since the early 1900s. He got his start as an enforcer for Italian gangs on the Lower East Side and had worked his way up to the position of crime boss. The veteran gangster had survived numerous assassination attempts and viewed himself as the rightful Mob leader in New York City.

Although they hated each other, Masseria and Maranzano had more in common than they would admit. Both men were considered to be "Mustache Petes" — a derisive name given to any old-time crime boss with conservative ideals. Mustache Petes were clannish and wanted to do business with fellow Italians only. They tended to move and act cautiously, to the irritation of younger, more aggressive gangsters such as Charles Luciano — one of Masseria's underlings who was chomping at the bit.

Within a few months of the Atlantic City meeting, the Maranzano/Masseria rivalry had exploded into open warfare. The conciliatory talk that had characterized the conference came to naught as the two mobsters fought an all-out war to the death. The streets of New York ran red with blood as gangsters blasted each other with pistols, sawed-off shotguns, and Tommy guns.

This battle of wills and weapons was dubbed the "Castellammarese War," because Maranzano and many of his henchmen came from Castellammare del Golfo, a town in Sicily. Both sides "went to the mattresses" — that is, established secret locales where their hit men would live, sleep, and eat when not gunning one another down.

While they sometimes acted like corporate executives, most gangsters preferred to settle disputes with rapid-fire machine guns instead of lawsuits. Issuing a "contract" did not have the same meaning in the underworld that it did in the boardroom. As future Mob bosses Lucky Luciano and Meyer Lansky would soon realize, it was extremely difficult to get undereducated, hyper-violent Mob leaders to work together peacefully.

Schultz hoped to sit out the Castellammarese War, but found himself sucked into the conflict anyway, due to his working relationship with Luciano. Because Luciano was connected with Masseria, it was assumed that Schultz supported

Joe the Boss. This automatically made Schultz an enemy of Maranzano and all his foot soldiers.

The Dutchman didn't care. He wasn't interested in the war between Masseria and Maranzano. His primary concern was growing the rackets he controlled. As Maranzano and Joe the Boss fought it out, Schultz — the lone wolf — took care of business and watched his profits soar. If he had thought his position through, he might have realized that even a lone wolf needs to run with the pack once in a while.

Chapter 3
Bullet Ballet

For all his success as a local crime boss, Schultz was still largely unknown to the press, public, and police outside of New York City. In 1931, all of that changed. This was the year that Schultz became famous nationwide. That he managed to survive the year is testament to his endurance and good fortune.

The Dutchman kicked things off with a fight at Club Abbey, a Manhattan nightclub on West 54th Street. On the evening of January 24, 1931, Schultz entered this establishment with one of his growing number of lieutenants, Marty Krompier, and business associate Larry Carney. Two women rounded out their entourage.

Schultz, now 28 years old, was just as homely and

disheveled as he had been before his rise to fame. Like any red-blooded male Mob boss, however, he enjoyed the company of attractive women. Appearances aside, the Dutchman had a fair bit to offer femme fatales who entered his orbit. Apart from the obvious attributes of wealth and power, he had a quirky charm and enjoyed living it up. A night on the town with Schultz was usually a memorable experience — and the evening at Club Abbey was no exception.

Schultz and his entourage took a corner table and ordered drinks. At some point Rene Bonnie, a female entertainer in the nightclub, sauntered over and joined the group. Krompier asked the delectable damsel to dance and they were soon waltzing around the dance floor. Their twirling came to an abrupt halt when a woman approached Rene and began to argue with her. Krompier added his voice to the argument, and Carney and the excitable Schultz hurried over to join in.

The unidentified woman was not alone. She had come to the club with Charles "Chink" Sherman, an associate of Waxey Gordon, who was a rival bootlegger of the Dutchman's. Sherman had some buddies with him and they leapt to defend their boss's moll.

In a flash, two packs of gangsters stood toe-to-toe, hissing and snarling at each other like wolverines. Other dancers gave the mobsters a wide berth. To no one's surprise, the cursing and threats gave way to blows. Schultz grabbed a chair and clocked Sherman on the head. Tables were overturned in the mêlée, and glasses, bottles, and dishes went flying. The nightclub took on the feel of a Wild West saloon as the two sides went at it. While Sherman was sprawled on the floor, Krompier grabbed a shard of glass and stabbed him. For good measure, someone — maybe Schultz, maybe Krompier — slashed Sherman's face with a broken beer bottle.

Seeing that his boss was down, one of Sherman's cronies pulled out his gun and started shooting. Amidst screams and shouts, Schultz and his crew made a dash for the door. Although he was wearing a bulletproof vest, Schultz had been pegged in the shoulder. It was time to call it a night.

By the time the cops arrived, the Dutchman and his crew were long gone, but Sherman could barely move. Showing little sympathy for the man's injuries, the police questioned him. Between groans, Sherman told them he had no idea who had attacked him. The frustrated cops had better luck questioning the other nightclubbers — many of whom had clearer recollections. However, while the clubbers were happy to describe the battle in vivid detail, they balked when it came to providing names. No one seemed to know the identity of the mysterious band of assailants who had put Sherman out of commission.

Schultz knew he was a prime suspect, but figured out a way to clear his name. In April, a few months after the skirmish, he brazenly challenged the police to prove he had been the assailant. It was all a grand game for the Dutchman because he knew that no one — not even the badly injured

Sherman — would identify him to the cops. The police hauled Schultz before a parade of witnesses who had been present at Club Abbey when the brawl had broken out. As Schultz predicted, none of them would identify him as the man who'd led the charge against Chink Sherman. The fuming cops had to let Schultz go.

Police fumbling aside, the Dutchman did not have an easy convalescence. His shoulder wound wasn't giving him much trouble, but Vincent Coll was. The mercurial henchman had suddenly decided he deserved more power and authority within the Schultz organization. He informed his employer he wanted to be treated like a full partner, sharing power equally with Schultz.

This proposal did not go over well. In the three years since Noe had died, Schultz had been the undisputed leader of his organization — and he wanted to keep it that way. Schultz had risen to his current status through a combination of guts, audacity, and a few lucky breaks. He enjoyed his wealth and power and had no intention of giving up cash and clout to this unhinged pretty-boy. Furthermore, Schultz had serious misgivings about Coll's managerial skills. While he was terrific when it came to maiming and killing people, the golden-haired gunman had shown little aptitude for deal-making and leadership. Also, Coll was a difficult man to like. His extremely impulsive behavior made even his toughest comrades nervous.

Schultz informed Coll that a promotion was not in the

works. The moody mobster would remain a foot soldier in the Dutchman's army of goons. Furious, Coll hurled abuse at his boss. As he left the premises, he shouted his intention to strike out on his own.

Unlike crime bosses such as Al Capone (who once beat three errant associates to death with a baseball bat), Schultz ruled with a relatively light touch. That is to say, he wasn't in the habit of killing or mauling staffers who displeased him — at least, not yet.

Still, Schultz had his limits. He knew he had to come down hard on Coll, the first man to openly challenge his leadership. As Schultz fumed and plotted, Coll added gas to the fire by screwing his ex-boss in court.

Prior to his split from Schultz, Coll had been charged with violating the Sullivan Law, a piece of legislation that made it illegal to carry a concealed weapon. Schultz had paid the $10,000 bail so Coll wouldn't have to remain in prison before the trial. The tight-fisted Schultz had been less than thrilled about forking over this cash, but had consoled himself with the thought that he'd eventually get his bail money back once Coll went on trial.

When Coll's case finally came up, however, the handsome hood didn't appear in court to enter a plea. Faced with a disappearing defendant, the court forfeited Coll's bail, thus leaving Schultz on the hook for 10 grand. The Dutchman just about swallowed his gray fedora when he heard about Coll's vanishing act. Any thoughts of mollifying his hot-tempered triggerman immediately went out the window. Coll and Schultz were soon at war — with predictably grim results.

On May 31, Schultz ordered his soldiers to gun down one of his own men — Vincent's brother. Peter Coll had never given Schultz any trouble, but his past loyalty and good record meant nothing to the Dutchman. Peter was Vincent's kin, so he had to die.

Even though Vincent Coll was a mean-hearted thug, he was devastated by his brother's death. He didn't mourn for long, however. In June, Coll went on a reckless rampage against his former boss. First, he hijacked Schultz's beer trucks, then, one by one, he killed four members of Schultz's gang. Schultz reached new levels of fury as he raged against his backstabbing ex-employee. He seemed prepared to kill Coll with his bare hands if given the chance.

Just as his feud with Coll kicked into high gear, Schultz acquired a new, more dangerous, enemy. This enemy was none other than Salvatore Maranzano, the boss who had come out on top in the Castellammarese War. That battle for the Mob's top spot had recently ended, thanks to some decisive action on the part of Charles Luciano.

Though Luciano worked for Giuseppe Masseria, he despised the older man because he was a Mustache Pete. Luciano wanted to kill Masseria, then take down the other old-timers. Around the time Coll and Schultz were exchanging insults, Luciano lured Masseria to an Italian restaurant on Coney Island. During dinner, Luciano excused himself and went to the washroom. At that moment, four of Luciano's men charged into the dining area and shot Joe the Boss Masseria to pieces. Masseria's death meant that Maranzano became *capo di tutti capi* … for the time being.

In victory, Maranzano proved be a sore winner. He held a grudge against all of Masseria's former friends and allies and wanted to annihilate them. Being an astute man, Maranzano was particularly eager to rid himself of his new ally, Luciano, along with Luciano's lieutenant, Vito Genovese. Maranzano's death list also included Joe Adonis, Frank Costello — and Dutch Schultz.

After proclaiming himself boss of all bosses, Maranzano contracted Schultz's nemesis to take out these gang leaders. Vincent Coll was delighted. Being paid to kill such high-level gangsters was exciting enough, but rubbing out Schultz would make the hits even sweeter. He decided to take his time and choose the right moment.

It's likely that Schultz didn't know about Maranzano's scheming, but he was well aware that Coll wanted him dead. However, he wasn't about to change his lifestyle because of their ongoing feud. Instead of going into hiding, Schultz seemed even more determined to enjoy his wealth and live the good life. While he wasn't interested in buying a new wardrobe, Schultz did want to live in a manner befitting a big-time crime boss.

In June, Schultz moved into a swanky ninth floor apartment on Fifth Avenue in Manhattan. The apartment was located near Central Park in an exclusive neighborhood. Not one to miss a trick, the Dutchman took the precaution of registering the apartment under the name Russell Jones.

Alas, the brawl at Club Abbey had greatly raised Schultz's public profile. An anonymous caller informed the police that Mr. Jones was none other than Dutch Schultz, one of the city's top mobsters.

Two police detectives — Stephen DiRosa and Julius Salke — were assigned to stake out Schultz's new digs. During the night of June 18, 1931, just days after Schultz had moved in, DiRosa and Salke sat down on a park bench across from the Dutchman's domicile. In plain clothes, but not trying to hide, they stayed at their post and kept their binoculars focused on the windows of Schultz's apartment.

The appearance of two inquisitive strangers outside his building in the middle of the night disconcerted the Dutchman. He watched the watchers and cursed.

Around 6 a.m., Schultz decided he'd had enough. Flanked by an associate named Danny Iamascia and two other thugs, he left the apartment and confronted the detectives. When the four toughs demanded to know what was going on, the detectives identified themselves as New York City police officers and informed Schultz that he was under police surveillance.

Iamascia smelled a rat. He figured the men weren't cops, but assassins sent by Coll to kill Schultz. As Iamascia glowered, Detective DiRosa drew his revolver. Eager to protect his boss, Iamascia pulled out his own pistol. DiRosa fired at point-blank range and hit Iamascia in the stomach and left wrist. As the wounded man sank to the ground, Schultz and his two remaining goons fled.

The two thugs dashed into Central Park and disappeared. Schultz, choosing a different escape route, began running towards 101st Street. He took out his .38 caliber revolver as he sprinted.

Schultz's chest grew tighter with each yard, but he still hoped to get away — until a bullet zinged by his head and he heard Detective Salke's authoritative voice demanding that he surrender. Panting, the Dutchman stopped in his tracks and let his gun fall to the ground.

Slouching toward Salke, hands raised high, Schultz turned on the charm and assured Salke and DiRosa that he didn't fight cops. The Dutchman complained that he was being "followed by mobsters" and that his life was in danger. He even asked if the detectives would help him. The cops snorted in derision. They couldn't tell if he was mocking them or truly wanted police protection.

The detectives demanded to know the identity of the badly wounded thug writhing on the ground back at the bench. Schultz played dumb and denied knowing him. When the cops warned him that his friend was dying, Schultz grudgingly gave up Danny Iamascia's name and urged the police to get a doctor. The Dutchman seemed shaken by Iamascia's obviously critical condition. The police didn't have time to find out if Schultz was putting them on or not.

The cops flagged down a cab. Identifying themselves as policemen, they picked up Iamascia and laid him on the floor of the taxi. Then they pushed Schultz into the backseat, got in beside him, and ordered the startled driver to take them to the nearest hospital. The cabbie shuddered and sped off.

As Iamascia moaned and bled by the men's feet, Schultz tried a new tactic. He offered each cop $50,000 plus a fancy home in a wealthy community if they would let him go. Unfortunately for Schultz, the detectives could not be bribed. They dumped Iamascia off at Mount Sinai Hospital, then ordered the dazed cabbie to drive to the police station on 104th Street. There, Schultz was officially charged with felonious assault and carrying a concealed weapon. The whole experience had greatly unnerved the excitable Dutchman. He asked for a sedative to calm him down.

When the police searched Schultz, they found he was carrying a small fortune. He had nearly $19,000 in his pockets, much of it in the form of $500 and $100 bills. Evidently, his bribe offer hadn't been a bluff.

During the interrogation, Schultz again denied knowing who Danny Iamascia was, even though he had identified the man to Salke and DiRosa earlier that day. He even claimed he hadn't dropped a gun during his chase. This was typical gangster behavior. When confronted by the law, gangsters would deny anything and everything, even though it often made them look ridiculous. The police gave Schultz a stern warning to appear in court when his trial came up, then let him go on bail.

Meanwhile, at Mount Sinai Hospital it looked as though Iamascia was not going to get off so easily. Despite doctors' best efforts, he died one day after the shootout.

Iamascia's death was marked by one of the gaudiest funerals ever thrown by the underworld. The gangster had been well respected in Mob circles, having racked up an impressive 10 arrests in six years. Gang leaders outdid themselves to honor his memory, all sending enormous floral tributes. One of the most striking floral attractions consisted of a 10-foot-high gate of lilies, roses, and carnations. Schultz's floral tribute was considerably smaller — and cheaper. It consisted of a tasteful arrangement of white roses arrayed around a cross. The word "sympathy" was spelled out at the bottom of the bouquet.

Thousands of people attended the funeral service, which was held at Our Lady of Carmel Church. The procession to St. Raymond's Cemetery consisted of more than 100 cars, 35 of which carried flowers instead of passengers. It was a magnificent send-off for a low-life thug.

Schultz's trial began a few weeks after his early morning encounter with the two detectives. Police took no chances with security. Authorities posted dozens of cops at the courthouse to make sure that none of the Dutchman's enemies tried to turn him into a dead defendant.

To the cops' chagrin, Schultz easily beat the rap on the

assault charge. The jury said the state couldn't prove that Schultz had aimed his gun in the direction of Detectives Salke and DiRosa. The Dutchman produced some sort of license that gave him the right to carry a gun, so authorities threw in the towel on the weapons charge, too. Salke and DiRosa were livid, but there was nothing the court could do.

After Schultz was acquitted, a big legal battle broke out over the $19,000 stash police had taken from him. The Dutchman's attorneys said the money belonged to Larry Carney, a member of the Schultz gang. Schultz insisted he had been merely hanging onto the cash, waiting for an opportunity to hand it over to Carney.

An unlikely story, but the courts ruled in Schultz's favor anyway. Since the police couldn't prove that the money was derived from the proceeds of a crime, legal authorities said they had no right to hold it. The defeated cops were forced to return the $19,000 to Shultz. They didn't ask if he passed it on to Carney.

During the time Schultz was on trial, Vincent Coll stopped harassing him. Once the court cases were over, however, Coll began scheming again. But before he could deliver a blow to his former boss, he had a more pressing problem to attend to.

The golden-haired gunman had managed to form a gang but, just as Schultz had predicted, proved to be a lousy businessman. By mid-1931, Coll's gang was broke. To finance their operations, Coll decided a little kidnapping was in order. His crew drove to Club Argonaut on Seventh Avenue and kidnapped George "Big Frenchy" DeMange at gunpoint. DeMange was a close friend of the wealthy Owney "Killer" Madden. Even though he was a major gangster with several murders to his credit, Madden had a soft spot for his buddies. He quickly paid a $35,000 ransom to release DeMange.

Coll didn't seem bothered by the fact that he had just crossed one of New York City's most well established crime figures. With the ransom money, Coll had plenty of cash to provide food, shelter, and high-powered weaponry for his crew. Once his gang's survival needs were taken care of, Coll launched a new phase in his campaign against Schultz.

On July 28, 1931, Coll and his assistants went on the hunt for members of Schultz's gang. The day was a scorcher. The U.S. northeast had been enduring a brutal heat wave, and dozens of people had already died from the heat. The death toll was about to climb.

Coll and four cronies were packed into a car as it slowly made its way down the streets of East Harlem. The car moved at a snail's space, as if the engine would blow from overexertion if it strained itself. All five occupants were sweating heavily. They constantly flicked back their hair and mopped their brows. With moist fingers, they fiddled with the guns in their laps.

Because of the heat, the sidewalks were filled with little kids playing in the bright sunshine. The youngsters ignored the touring car as it made its way down East 107th Street. It was just another car, driving sluggishly in the warm air.

The vehicle ambled along the sticky asphalt until it reached the Helmar Social Club. As the men in the car knew, the Helmar was a known hangout for Joey Rao, one of Schultz's associates. Sure enough, Rao was standing in front of the club taking in the sun. Rao didn't seem any more interested in the approaching vehicle than the kids were. The car drew up alongside Rao and slowed until it had almost stopped.

A shotgun and a .45 automatic suddenly appeared in the open windows of the vehicle. The street echoed with the sound of gunfire and children's screams. At the first shot, Rao dove for cover. Bullets zipped around him as he desperately tried to get out of the line of fire. After the fusillade, the car raced off, leaving five squirming bodies on the sidewalk. Rao, shaken but unhurt, looked at the victims in horror. Coll's gang had hit five innocent children.

Parents screamed and raced toward the Helmar Social Club, praying their children were alive. Four of the wounded survived. Michael Vengalli, a five-year-old, died the next day.

Rao quickly made himself scarce. He wasn't about to report his near-assassination to the cops. Fortunately, the police didn't need Rao to break the case. Probably because the crime was so appalling, a witness came forward to identify the gunmen. The eyewitness, whose name was George Brecht, identified two of the assailants as Vincent Coll and Frank Giordano.

The press began baying for blood. They labeled Coll the "Baby Killer" and called him a "Mad Dog." A nationwide manhunt soon ensued. Coll dyed his blond hair black, grew a mustache, and went into hiding. He didn't have many friends to turn to — even his fellow gangsters were disgusted by his actions.

A failure as a Mob boss, and now a hunted man, Coll gave up on his quest for revenge for the time being. Far from harming Schultz, by hurting innocent children he had actually made the Dutchman look good by comparison.

Dutch Schultz had won this round by a knockout.

Chapter 4
The Long Arm
of the Dutchman

After winning the brutal Castellammarese War, Salvatore Maranzano turned unexpectedly conciliatory toward Lucky Luciano and Vito Genovese. In early September 1931, the new *capo di tutti capi* asked them to come to a meeting at his office in the New York Central Building on Park Avenue.

Maranzano's plan was that Vincent Coll — who was still hiding from police — would show up during the meeting and plug Lucky and Vito full of lead. But fortune smiled on its namesake when Lucky discovered the true purpose of the tête-à-tête. Having disposed of one old-school Mob boss, Luciano had few qualms about killing another Mustache Pete, especially one who had intended to double-cross him.

Luciano had a few gangsters dress in police uniforms

— or as IRS agents according to other accounts — and sent them to the sit-down in his place. On September 10, 1931, these fake lawmen marched into the New York Central Building and blasted Maranzano to eternity. For good measure, they also stabbed him and slashed his throat. By the time Mad Dog Coll arrived on the scene, the hit squad had fled and his sponsor was nothing more than a blood-soaked corpse.

Maranzano's death meant that Schultz, who had been on the old man's death list, was now safe. It also meant that Luciano could step into the position of top Mob *capo* in New York City.

Luciano had not respected Maranzano, but he was impressed by his vision of an organized, structured Mob. Maranzano's dream had extended no farther than New York City's municipal boundaries; Luciano wanted to expand on that idea. He envisioned a national regulatory body that would bring order and discipline to the freewheeling underworld across the entire United States.

Working with Meyer Lansky, Luciano began setting up a criminal leadership board called the Commission. Also given the grander name of the National Crime Syndicate, the Commission would eventually include top-ranking Italian and Jewish gangsters such as Frank Costello, Joe Adonis, Meyer Lansky, and Longy Zwillman.

Dutch Schultz was not part of the Commission's inner circle. While recognized as a major crime boss, he was far too independent and impulsive to submit to the will of a criminal collective. The new Mob organization preferred to deal with team players. Besides, some of the crime lords were wary of Schultz's eccentricities and considered him a bit of an outsider. If the Dutchman rocked the boat, it would be at his own peril.

While Luciano was overseeing his grand plan, Vincent Coll was still trying to elude authorities. Since the failed assassination attempt on Luciano, Coll also had to worry about retribution from the new boss of all bosses, as well as from his old nemesis Schultz. The fugitive's dyed hair and new mustache didn't fool the police for long. He was picked up on October 4, just a few weeks after the debacle in Maranzano's office, and police slapped him with murder charges for the July gun rampage at the Helmar Social Club.

Mad Dog Coll and the two other gunmen involved in the Helmar child slaying — Frank Giordano and Patsy Dugan — went on trial for killing Michael Vengali. One of New York's best defense attorneys, Samuel Leibowitz, defended the men. Amazingly, thanks to Leibowitz's slick work, Coll and his henchmen were acquitted of killing the child. Though Frank Giordano still faced another trial for an unrelated murder, Mad Dog Coll and Dugan were free men.

Coll took the opportunity to issue a histrionic statement to the press. It read: "I have been charged with all kinds of crimes but baby killing was the limit. I'd like nothing better than to lay my hands on the man who did this. I'd tear his throat out. There is nothing more despicable than a man who would harm an innocent child."

To celebrate his courtroom victory, Coll married his girlfriend, Lottie Kriesberger. The police interrupted their nuptials by arresting Mad Dog on a conspiracy beef. After spending his honeymoon behind bars, Coll finally made it back to the arms of his passionate bride.

Once the police released him from custody, Coll tried to keep a low profile. He might have evaded the long arm of the law, but he knew the Dutchman's hounds had picked up his scent. In February 1932, Schultz discovered that Coll was scheduled to play cards with some buddies. The friendly card game was going to take place at a private residence on Commonwealth Avenue in the North Bronx. Schultz sent a posse of four thugs to liven up the game.

In one of the downstairs rooms in the small house, two men and a woman sat around a table staring at their cards. When Schultz's thugs kicked in the door, guns drawn, the players looked up in shock. Then they were blown to bits. It was no contest: Schultz's death squad fired so quickly that their startled quarry didn't have time to draw their weapons. The three card enthusiasts were slain where they sat. They fell out of their chairs and slumped to the floor amongst the scattered cards and poker chips.

With the reek of gunpowder and blood hanging in the air, the gunmen raced outside and piled into a getaway car. As they tore away from the scene of the crime, they wondered what their boss would have to say about their day's work.

They had blown away Patsy Dugan, Fiorio Basile (another of Coll's soldiers), and their friend Emily Torrizello. But not Vincent Coll. Just as he had in the Maranzano foul-up, the tardy dandy arrived on the scene after the party was over. Only the dead and wounded greeted him. Several other adults and four kids had been in the house during the hit. Of these, two adults were wounded, but the children were not harmed.

After his latest narrow escape, it's safe to say that Mad Dog — who was not the brightest star in the gangland universe — realized he was living on borrowed time. Indeed, within days of the failed assassination, Schultz tried again. This time, he made sure his prey was properly cornered first.

Coll was tracked down to the Cornish Arms Hotel on 23rd Street, where he was living with his new missus. Through a bit of scouting and skullduggery, it was determined that he was going to leave the hotel and use the phone in the nearby London Chemist pharmacy in the early hours of February 9.

Sure enough, at 12:30 a.m., Coll left his hotel and went into the pharmacy, accompanied by a bodyguard. Probably nervous to be out in public, even in the middle of the night, Coll cautiously maneuvered his way around counters and slid into a phone booth. He plunked some coins into the phone and dialed. It wasn't clear if Coll was making a prearranged call or was simply too paranoid to use the phone in his hotel in case the police had tapped the line.

About 10 minutes into Coll's conversation, a limousine carrying three men pulled up outside. Bo Weinberg, who was rapidly becoming Schultz's top enforcer, was driving. He stayed at the wheel and left the motor running as the two other occupants got out. One man stood watch by the curb while his partner sauntered into the pharmacy with a Thompson machine gun plainly in sight. Even at that hour, there were customers in the store. The gunman simply told them to "keep cool" as he approached Coll's phone booth.

According to some sources, a terrified Coll yelled for his bodyguard. But that wouldn't have done him much good. Just as things started to get frantic inside the pharmacy, the bodyguard decided to take a hike. He slipped off the seat at the soda counter and casually strolled outside. The guard's laid-back air suggested he, too, was in on the hit. The bodyguard passed by the lookout at the curb and vanished.

Standing only a few feet away from his target, the gunman leveled his weapon and sprayed the phone booth with automatic fire. Mad Dog Coll didn't have a chance. As the U.S. military experts who developed the weapon noted, the Thompson machine gun was fantastically lethal at close range. It literally cut its victims apart. The only other gat that came close to the Tommy gun in terms of creating sheer carnage was a sawed off shotgun.

Coll took at least 15 rounds. The heavy slugs tore through his body and gouged huge holes in the wall behind him. By the time the shooting ended, the phone booth looked as though it had been hit with an artillery barrage.

With shell casings littering the floor, the machine-gunner raced out of the pharmacy. Corn plasters, cough syrup, and bandages fell from the shelves as he brushed against them in his haste. Horrified clerks and customers stared gap-jawed as the man ran past, still gripping his smoking Thompson.

Outside the pharmacy, Weinberg waited behind the wheel of the getaway car. Seeing the commotion inside the drugstore, the goon standing watch knew their mission had been accomplished. He dove into the vehicle, closely followed by the assassin. Weinberg gunned the engine, but he wasn't able to make a clean getaway.

As it turned out, Schultz's thugs had not been the only men tailing Vincent Coll that night. Two police detectives had been shadowing him and were waiting near the pharmacy. These cops came running the instant they heard the rolling thunder of the Tommy gun. They made it to the front of the London Chemist just as Weinberg drove off.

As soon as the detectives saw the speeding getaway car and the bullet-pocked interior of the drugstore, they knew they wouldn't have to follow Coll any longer. The cops lacked a car, but that didn't stop them from giving chase. In the kind of scene that Hollywood is so fond of recreating, one cop jumped on the running board of a cab and ordered the startled driver to "follow that car!" While hanging onto the vehicle with one hand, the plucky lawman fired at the weaving getaway car.

When he ran out of bullets, the officer waved his empty piece in the air. It took two hands to reload, and the cop wasn't about to remove his grip on the side of the taxi to put fresh rounds in his gun.

The getaway car and the taxicab did a frantic dance along Eighth Avenue. As shocked night owls looked on, the two vehicles darted in and out of traffic at speeds topping 60 miles an hour. Other cars honked their horns and slammed on their brakes to avoid being hit. Amazingly, the two vehicles didn't run into anyone.

The chase went on for a good 27 blocks, past sleepy drivers and startled pedestrians, before Weinberg managed to shake his pursuer. The grim-faced detective finally allowed the cabbie to stop. It's doubtful the taxi driver got a good tip for his efforts.

Vincent Coll hadn't been forgotten in all the excitement. His traitor bodyguard went to the Cornish Arms Hotel, where Coll's wife was waiting for her handsome husband to return. There, he informed her that Mad Dog had been shot. Why the guard passed on this information isn't clear. Perhaps he was trying to establish an underworld alibi that he had been outgunned and had to flee for his life.

After she heard the news, the former Miss Lottie Kriesberger went rushing to the London Chemist and burst through the crowd of gawkers and police. At the sight of the mangled corpse, the young woman began screaming hysterically. Coll was no longer handsome. The police allowed her to grieve for a minute then took her to the station. There, she became close-mouthed and refused to answer any questions about her husband and his associates.

Compared to Danny Iamascia's funeral, Coll's send-off was a flop. Barely 100 people attended the event, which was held at the Walter B. Cooke Funeral Home in the Bronx. Only immediate family members were present when the Dutchman's most volatile enemy was buried at St. Raymond's Cemetery.

The Dutchman had won the match.

Chapter 5
Lucky Numbers

Dutch Schultz grinned as he gazed at the nervous Puerto Rican seated across from him. The man, Jose Enrique "Henry" Miro, was one of the highest ranking figures in the Harlem "numbers" racket — Schultz's latest moneymaking venture. Miro avoided Schultz's unwavering stare by looking down and studying his pajama buttons. He had been in bed when the Dutchman's men summoned him to this late-night meeting. The prospect of going face-to-face with Schultz was so unnerving that he had not wasted time getting dressed.

As anxious as he was, Miro couldn't help noticing that Schultz looked a mess. He was wearing a cheap suit and dirty shirt, and his hair was greasy and askew. The fearful mobster even had food crumbs on his chin.

The Dutchman's grin changed to a smirk as he removed a .45 caliber automatic pistol from his belt. He casually laid the handgun on the desk between them then cracked his knuckles and leaned back in his chair. As Miro shivered, the Dutchman began to speak. He had a very specific message for Miro.

The first thing Schultz wanted was $500 a week, in "protection" money. Miro gulped and nodded his head. "Not a problem, not a problem," he said.

"And," continued the Dutchman, "I want you to stay out of Ison's turf. He's a friend of mine."

Once again, Miro assured Schultz that this would not be a problem. With nothing left to discuss, the Dutchman called the meeting to a close and let his latest business partner stumble back home.

This sort of late-night intimidation session was old hat to Schultz. But the numbers racket was a new venture for him. Branching out was a sign of the times. By mid-1932, Schultz and other far-seeing gangsters realized that Prohibition was coming to an end. Public sentiment had turned against the law — in large part because of the violence created by bootleggers like Schultz and Al Capone. Even supporters of Prohibition had to admit their attempt to make America "dry" had been a dismal failure.

To add to this, the United States was in the midst of a terrible economic downturn. The Great Depression had begun three years earlier when the New York City Stock

Market crashed. With mass unemployment and poverty, it seemed more important for the government to spend money on relief efforts than on stamping out booze. Mobsters began looking for new revenue streams.

Unlike his peers who jumped into gambling, prostitution, and narcotics, Schultz began to sniff out opportunities in the Harlem-based numbers racket. This was a sector that most of the Dutchman's compatriots sneeringly dismissed as not worthy of their time and talents. The numbers racket was largely dominated by African Americans, which probably added to the gangsters' disdain.

The numbers racket was nothing more than an illegal lottery. A penny or two bought you a "policy slip" (an illicit lottery ticket) containing a three-digit number from 0 to 999. Each day — or week, depending on who was running the game — a winning number would be selected. Winning numbers were usually based on stock market prices or horseracing results. If your number was selected — or "hit" in numbers lingo — you won a small amount of money.

The numbers racket was hugely popular among poor people, for obvious reasons. It was extremely cheap to play and the risks — to the players at least — were negligible. Practically everyone in Harlem played, from criminals and the desperately poor to respectable working people with solid jobs.

Policy slips were stored and sorted at "policy banks," which were set up in offices or warehouses. By the time

Schultz stepped onto the scene, there were more than two-dozen policy banks in Harlem. Each bank employed about 20 to 30 "runners" — minions who sold the policy slips and paid the winners. The boss in charge of the operation had the grand title of "policy banker."

Schultz's entrée into the numbers world was facilitated by Richard "Dixie" Davis, a flamboyant and extremely corrupt criminal lawyer. Not quite 30 years old, Davis had a predilection for fancy suits and expensive clothes. In court, he had a tendency to rant and scream, which endeared him to his uneducated clients.

Like Schultz, Davis was a self-made man who had been born into a poor family. More from desperation than desire, Davis found himself defending numbers runners after graduating from New York Law School in 1927. They were the only clients the struggling lawyer could find. By the time Schultz caught up to him, Davis had established himself as the busiest numbers attorney in New York. He had a large staff and handled the business of Harlem's top policy bankers.

Schultz sought out Davis and formed an alliance with him. With Davis at his side, the Dutchman went about trying to control the Harlem numbers racket. To achieve this, Schultz relied on a combination of threats, guile, political pressure, and insider information. It helped that numbers racketeers were not consolidated into one cohesive organization. Instead, they worked as independent operators, which made them easier to pick off. Nor were the policy bankers a particularly violent crew. Because so many respectable people played the numbers, the criminals who ran the racket rarely had to resort to force.

Schultz made his first move by inviting Alexander Pompez, a high profile Harlem policy banker, to a sit-down at the Oswasco Democratic Club on 118th Street. The club was affiliated with Tammany Hall, the corrupt municipal political machine, and was a cozy and convenient place for Schultz to hold his meetings.

The Dutchman did not face Pompez by himself. Also taking part in the meeting were his goons George Weinberg and Solly Girsch. These gentlemen convinced Pompez that it would be in his best interest to fork out weekly payments for protection. Pompez quickly caved in and left.

Within minutes, a second numbers man, Joseph Matthias "Spasm" Ison, was brought in and given the same spiel about protection money. Ison, who had earned his nickname because of the impressive facial tics he displayed when playing cards, wasn't persuaded as easily. He played for time then consulted his lawyer. To Ison's surprise, the lawyer, Dixie Davis, advised him to go along with the extortion scheme.

After some negotiation, Ison agreed to Schultz's terms, but he demanded a favor in return. Henry Miro was cutting into his turf, and Ison wanted him stopped. It was this business arrangement that led to the hapless Miro being summoned by the Dutchman in the middle of the night.

While he had successfully shaken down three of the

biggest players in the numbers scene, Schultz still faced significant opposition in the form of Stephanie St. Clair, a black woman known as the "Policy Queen of Harlem."

Tall, tough, and ruthless, St. Clair hailed from the French colony of Martinique, in the Caribbean. She had come to America shortly before World War I by way of Marseilles, France. The Policy Queen was one of very few females in top New York City crime circles. It was a sign of her leadership abilities and the power of her personality that she had risen to such heights.

According to underworld gossip, St. Clair had 40 runners in her employ and a personal fortune of around $500,000. The thought of taking over such a lucrative business made the Dutchman drool.

Strident and stubborn, the Policy Queen resisted all of Schultz's sleazy overtures. She wasn't interested in becoming business "partners" with Schultz or joining his underworld empire. When Schultz turned aggressive and began applying pressure, St. Clair remained defiant. In fact, she complained directly to the mayor and district attorney. She asked each man in turn to get Schultz to stop leaning on her. But neither the mayor nor the district attorney moved a finger to help St. Clair. Although she had been paying graft for years, city officials reckoned that Schultz had deeper pockets.

The Policy Queen had some built-in disadvantages as well. She was black and female, while Schultz was white and male — like most New Yorkers in positions of power. In the socially rigid climate of the day, the power brokers would naturally feel more kinship toward Schultz than St. Clair.

Schultz's main man on the political front was a West Side Tammany Hall fixture named James J. "Jimmy" Hines. The same year he moved into the numbers racket, Schultz established a profitable relationship with Hines, who was one of the most powerful political leaders in the city. Dutch enlisted Hines's aid in keeping the police heat off the numbers trade. In exchange, Schultz paid Hines several hundred tax-free dollars a week.

Undeterred by the politicians' lack of cooperation, St. Clair tried another strategy to combat Schultz. She attempted to get other Harlem policy bankers to forge an alliance against Schultz, but they wouldn't go along with her. She ran ads in local Harlem newspapers that openly detailed the Dutchman's machinations and the local political corruption that gave him so much pull in the city. The advertising campaign backfired — according to some accounts, angry authorities had the Policy Queen locked up for spilling the beans on municipal malfeasance. She was released after a few months, only to see Schultz seize control of her business.

Schultz muscled St. Clair aside, but he didn't have her assassinated. In fact, he let her continue running her business. This was typical of the way he operated in Harlem. Black policy bankers were allowed to keep operating, as long as they forked over most of their profits to Schultz and left him to make all the major decisions. The power-hungry mogul centralized operations and kept close tabs on the policy slips that continued to pour in.

If the Policy Queen was grateful to Schultz for keeping her alive, she didn't show it. St. Clair maintained a white-hot hatred for the cocky Schultz. She would never forgive the Dutchman and his rapacious ways.

Once he had complete control over the Harlem policy racket, Schultz became wealthier than he'd ever imagined. Each day, his various numbers games grossed roughly $35,000, about a quarter of which went to the winners. One estimate pegged the Dutchman's annual take from the policy trade at around $12 million to $14 million a year, a huge fortune during the Great Depression.

For all the money he was making from African Americans, Schultz harbored less than brotherly feelings toward his new business partners. In financial statements detailing income and expenses, Schultz referred to his black workers derogatorily. He also agreed to a plan to rig the numbers game to make it tougher to win.

The plan came from a man named Otto Berman. Berman had a body like a blimp and a mind like a computer. He liked to call himself "Abbadabba" because he was a mathematical genius, able to juggle complex numbers and figures in his head. Abbadabba was a highly successful gambler, with a particular propensity for choosing winning horses. Berman's big idea was to rig the payoffs from which the winning policy numbers were taken.

To determine the winning policy, bankers followed a complicated formula: they added up the cash payoffs for three series of horse races at a given track. Say these payoffs came to $125, $252, and $181. The bankers would take the third digit of each payoff (12<u>5</u>, 25<u>2</u> and 18<u>1</u>) and put them together for the winning policy (in this case, "521").

Everyone who had purchased a policy slip bearing the number 521 would be a winner. A penny bet would earn a few dollars. A dollar bet, obviously, would pay much more. If only a handful of people played the winning number, the policy bank would earn a healthy profit. But if lots of people played that number, the bank would have to fork over a fortune in winnings. Policy bankers lived in dread of the day when a popular number "hit."

This is where Abbadabba Berman came in. Each day, Berman would troop out to one of the racetracks where policy numbers were derived. These tracks were located as far afield as Florida or Ohio.

Berman would watch a few races and then phone a Schultz associate in New York to find out what the most popular numbers were that day. After receiving this information, Berman would calculate the odds in various upcoming races then place a bunch of last-minute bets. His intention was to alter the payoffs so that heavily played numbers didn't hit.

This scheme was mind-bogglingly complex, but it worked. Berman soon increased the Dutchman's profit margin

by a healthy share. Abbadabba himself became the benefi-
ciary of a $10,000 a week salary, courtesy of Schultz. Numbers
players in Harlem continued to purchase policy slips, totally
unaware that their chances of winning were becoming
increasingly slimmer.

The same year that Schultz took over the numbers racket, he also got into a seemingly legitimate enterprise — the
restaurant business.

A Schultz lieutenant named Julius Modgilewsky spear-
headed Schultz's entrance into the world of dining establishments. Modgilewsky, who preferred to be called "Modgilewsky
the Commissar" or, just simply, Jules Martin, purchased
a dingy diner in town. Martin had no intention of fixing
the place up; he merely wanted to use the eatery to gain a
foothold in Local 16 of the Hotel and Restaurant Employees
International Alliance. This union oversaw waiters working
north of 14th Street in Manhattan.

With Schultz's approval, Martin moved to take over
Local 16. Martin arranged for Mob men to run for union
office and used illegal electoral tricks to help them win.
Ballot stuffing and intimidation at the polls led Martin's representatives to victory. Martin's candidates were so successful
that they received more votes than there were members of
the union.

Next, the Schultz/Martin team decided to take over
Local 302 of the Delicatessen Counterman and Cafeteria
Workers Union. This time, they didn't even bother running

candidates. They simply threatened to harm the leaders of the union if they didn't join forces with the mobsters. The union bosses were eager to comply.

After taking over the two locals, Martin and another Schultz associate, Sam Krantz, focused their attention on management. The two formed something called "The Metropolitan Restaurant & Cafeteria Owners Association." In theory, the association was supposed to represent the interests of hard-pressed restaurateurs. In practice, the organization existed so that the Schultz group could extract dues from their unlucky members.

Association officials went on an aggressive membership drive. Their tactics amounted to pure blackmail. Metropolitan representatives would contact restaurant owners and tell them that the waiters' union, which Schultz controlled, was demanding a 200 percent increase in the wages of their wait staff. This huge wage increase could be avoided, however, if the restaurateur joined the Metropolitan Restaurant & Cafeteria Owners Association.

If the owners balked, they would find their wait staff walking off the job. Thanks to their control of the waiters' and deli workers' unions, Schultz's men could order strikes whenever they wanted. Such pressure tactics were highly effective in convincing restaurant owners to join Schultz's bogus organization. To add insult to injury, the unfortunate owners had to sign documents stating that they were joining the Metropolitan Association of their own free will.

New members faced a sliding scale of fees. Smaller cafeterias might get away with paying a $250 initiation fee and $30 a year in annual dues. Bigger, more established places would have to pay initiation fees that ran anywhere from $5000 to $25,000, plus dues.

Anyone who resisted this extortion would be stink-bombed out of business. Typically tossed down a chimney or through a window, the stink bombs used by the Schultz gang were made from butyric acid. When these bombs exploded, they permeated the air — and everything in their vicinity — with a terrible stench. Drapes, carpets, wood, and even cement would take on a foul odor that was almost impossible to get rid of. Meanwhile, the acid in the bombs destroyed expensive tables and fixtures. Faced with an offensively odoriferous establishment, holdout restaurateurs were forced into bankruptcy. The mere threat of being stink-bombed was enough to convince most restaurant owners to capitulate.

While never as big as numbers, the restaurant racket provided Schultz with a healthy income, to the tune of about $2 million a year.

The Dutchman's life wasn't all about business, however. At some point in 1932, he met a young, attractive redhead who worked as a hatcheck girl at the Maison Royal nightclub. Her name was Frances Geis, but she also went by Frances Maxwell. She was a mere teenager —18 years of age. Schultz was 12 years her senior. It's questionable whether the young woman was really impressed by the Dutchman's good manners and "unpretentious" clothing, as she later claimed to have been, or whether she recognized a good financial opportunity when she saw one. In any case, Frances and Schultz soon became an item.

While Schultz seemed to genuinely love Frances, he never introduced her to his mother. Perhaps he was embarrassed by the fact that she was very young — and a Christian to boot. A good Jewish mom, Mrs. Flegenheimer wouldn't appreciate her only son going out with a *shiksa.*

Of course, Schultz might have also withheld an introduction simply because it never crossed his mind to let his mother know he had a girlfriend. Unlike Al Capone, who financially supported his mother, brothers, and sisters, Schultz remained somewhat aloof from his roots. He didn't shower his family with money or buy houses for them. In fact, Schultz didn't even like to talk about his childhood. When anyone broached the topic, he was usually curt and dismissive. According to some accounts, Schultz hated to reminisce about his upbringing because it brought back memories of his disappearing father.

For her part, Mrs. Flegenheimer appears to have remained devoted to her distant son. If she was oblivious of her little Arthur's love life, she was equally ignorant about his business affairs. Apparently, Schultz never told his mother that he was a gangster during the infrequent moments when he communicated with her. How she failed to realize that the infamous Dutch Schultz was, in fact, her Arthur isn't clear.

Dutch kept in slightly closer contact with his sister, Helen. Unlike his mother, his sister was more clued in about Schultz's criminal activities. During Prohibition, Schultz gave Helen's husband, Henry Orsprung, a job looking after the vending machines in his speakeasies. As a result of this gig, Henry acquired the nickname "Peanuts." Later, Schultz put Henry to work as a low-level official in the numbers racket. This was about as magnanimous as Schultz ever got with his family.

The Dutchman was always more concerned about growing his own pot of cash than in sharing the wealth. By late 1932, his fortune had grown prodigiously. In fact, he was on something of a personal and professional roll. All the troubles of the previous year were distant memories.

Schultz could choose to ignore little bumps in the road, such as the abrupt resignation of gangster-friendly mayor Jimmy Walker. Earlier in the decade, the New York State Legislature had launched an investigation to uncover municipal corruption in New York City. Walker found himself under intense scrutiny, accused of accepting hundreds of thousands of dollars in bribes. Before he could be officially charged with anything, Walker suddenly quit and fled to Europe in September 1932.

Walker's replacement was a nonentity named John O'Brien. O'Brien's main concern was expanding the city's tax base and putting New York on solid financial footing. Meanwhile, in the background, an ambitious crime-busting ex-congressman by the name of Fiorello LaGuardia was chomping at the bit to get into the mayor's chair.

While all these changes were going on at city hall, other forces were mustering their strength to do battle with the Dutchman. A federal grand jury in New York was slowly gathering evidence of his malfeasance. A grand jury is a force to be reckoned with. Made up of private citizens, its sole function is to investigate whether enough evidence exists against a suspect to issue an indictment. If a grand jury were to indict Schultz, it would become the responsibility of a trial jury to weigh his innocence or guilt. Launched in mid-1931, the federal grand jury was interested in Mr. Flegenheimer's income tax returns, or lack thereof. The authorities hoped to nail Schultz on income tax evasion — the same charge that brought down Al Capone in the fall of 1931.

Tax evasion was one of the very few charges that gave gangsters pause. Unlike murder, which could always be portrayed as "self-defense," it was hard for mobsters to explain why they didn't file proper tax returns.

The legal eagle behind the grand jury was an intense, mustachioed young man named Thomas Dewey. Dewey had been born in Michigan in 1902 — the same year as Arthur Flegenheimer — and took a law degree at Columbia University. After graduating, the serious-minded lawyer became a chief assistant to the United States Attorney for the Southern District of New York.

Dewey was highly ambitious and incorruptible — a

dangerous combination for Dutch Schultz. By presenting mounds of evidence and countless witnesses, Dewey hoped to convince the grand jury that the Dutchman had failed to do his duty as an American citizen by not paying the taxes he owed Uncle Sam.

Dutch's lucky days were numbered.

Chapter 6
Public Enemy
Number One

Dutch Schultz's good fortune came to a jarring end on January 25, 1933, when the federal grand jury investigating his finances indicted him for tax evasion. A criminal trial would be forthcoming. Thomas Dewey felt he was well on his way to putting the Dutchman behind bars.

While Dewey was aware that Schultz had his finger in several criminal pies, he focused on the most visible of the Dutchman's illicit enterprises — bootlegging. According to the circumspect lawyer, Schultz hadn't filed tax returns for 1929, 1930, and 1931, even though he had earned an estimated $481,637.35 from bootlegging during this time. This very precise figure must actually have been an educated guess. But if this was indeed Schultz's income, he owed the federal government $92,103.34 in uncollected taxes — a stiff figure even for a high-rolling gangster. Not only was Schultz liable for this debt, he faced a huge fine, and, potentially, 43 years in prison.

The charges must have deeply stung the Dutchman. While his personal wealth was estimated at around $7 million, Schultz remained cheap to the point of miserliness. He still liked to boast that he never paid more than $2 for a shirt or $35 for an off-the-rack suit. Prices in the 1930s were a fraction of what they are today, but two bucks was still a bargain-basement price for a shirt.

As Lucky Luciano commented in a later reminiscence, "Schultz was one of the cheapest guys I ever knew ... here was a guy with a couple of million bucks and he dressed like a pig. His big deal was buyin' a newspaper for two cents so he could read all about himself."

So, no one was surprised when the stingy Schultz announced he wasn't going to pay his tax bill. The Dutchman took a good look at the legal landscape and went into hiding.

Within a few days of the indictment, Schultz became a fugitive. The police distributed 50,000 "Wanted" posters featuring Schultz's pasty mug, but they were unable to track him down. The inability of law officers to find the Dutchman was quite remarkable, considering he didn't exactly keep a low profile.

In fact, Schultz was regularly seen about town, traveling between his various residences and the headquarters of the policy rackets in Harlem. He also regularly visited his girl-friend, frequented nightclubs and restaurants, and patronized a mid-Manhattan house of prostitution.

The Dutchman could get away with such brazen acts of defiance because of his clout with local politicians, especially Jimmy Hines. During 1933, city government was still dominated by corrupt Tammany Hall — although that was soon to change. Many local politicos enjoyed the largesse of gangsters such as Schultz and had no intention of bringing him — or any other high-ranking mobsters — to justice.

Still, for all the protection Schultz could buy from local police and their political masters, he wasn't safe. The grand jury case was not going to go away and honest authorities such as Thomas Dewey were determined to nab him.

Knowing that the law would eventually catch up with him, the Dutchman played for time. He needed money to fund his defense, but unfortunately, one of his regular revenue streams was about to dry up.

In early 1933, the newly elected President Franklin Roosevelt modified the Volstead Act to make it legal to drink low-alcohol (3.2 percent) beer. A few months later, "real" beer had become legal as well. At the same time, a constitutional amendment to repeal federal prohibition was gaining ground in state legislatures. If two-thirds of the states supported the measure, a prospect that looked more certain every day, Prohibition would be repealed. American citizens were delighted. It would only be a matter of time before hard liquor was again legalized.

Although Schultz had foreseen this and successfully moved into the numbers and restaurant rackets, he still derived a healthy portion of his income from bootlegging — a fact duly noted by the grand jury.

During this period, Schultz also spent a lot of time and money trying to get William Copeland Dodge elected as district attorney for Manhattan. Hines had suggested that Dodge was the perfect candidate for DA. If the Dutchman helped fund his election campaign, the elderly Dodge could be counted on to overlook Schultz's criminal activities.

Dixie Davis, Schultz's sharp lawyer, expressed concerns that Dodge was too stupid for the post. Hines, however, assured Schultz that he could control Dodge, and with Schultz's assistance, Dodge narrowly won the election.

Three weeks before Christmas 1933, Utah became the 36th state to approve the constitutional proposal to gut Prohibition. The Volstead Act was voided as federal prohibition officially came to an end.

As if this wasn't bad enough, the Dutchman was soon dealt another blow. Another principled politician was out to get him. His name was Fiorello Henry LaGuardia, and he had finally won the mayor's job.

Of mixed Italian and Jewish heritage, LaGuardia went by the nickname "Little Flower," which is the literal English translation of Fiorello. As a congressman in the 1920s, LaGuardia had repeatedly spoken out against Prohibition and the crime it generated. While on the mayoral campaign trail, LaGuardia had bitterly denounced city hall corruption and organized crime.

Like Dewey, LaGuardia was genuinely disgusted with the criminal underworld and its ability to manipulate legal and political institutions. He was determined to set a new tone for city government. On his first day in office, LaGuardia made a stirring radio address to the nation. "New York City was restored to the people this morning, at one minute after midnight," said the Little Flower in his address. "It is my duty from now on to guard and protect and guide the complete, peaceful and undisturbed enjoyment of that possession."

LaGuardia took personal aim at certain local gangsters, including Schultz. The new mayor ordered police to seize the illegal slot machines that the Dutchman had installed in various establishments around town. As the press looked on, the Little Flower took a sledgehammer and smashed these machines to bits. Other slot machines were thrown into the East River. Schultz was enraged, but he couldn't do anything about it. Even for a gangster of Schultz's status, it would be suicide to threaten the mayor of New York City.

Although his empire seemed to be crumbling, it wasn't all doom and gloom for Schultz. To the surprise of his cronies, the Dutchman developed an interest in spiritual matters. He had always been a non-practicing Jew, but now he began delving into Catholic rituals and beliefs. Something about Catholicism fascinated him. He even toyed with the idea of converting. On top of this spiritual renaissance, Schultz experienced another transformation: he became a father.

On June 26, 1934, Frances, who was now calling herself Schultz's wife even though they weren't legally married, gave birth to a girl. The happy parents named their daughter Anne Davis Flegenheimer — the "Davis" being in honor of Dixie Davis. Like all new parents, they looked forward to watching the girl grow up.

This period of calm domesticity did not last long, however. With the new squeaky-clean mayor in town, federal authorities continued to strike hard against the Dutchman.

In late 1934, Henry Morgenthau Jr. (President Roosevelt's Secretary of the Treasury) put in phone calls to Mayor LaGuardia and J. Edgar Hoover — head of the Federal Bureau of Investigation (FBI). Arthur Flegenheimer was the subject of both calls. Morgenthau told LaGuardia that they had a "common interest" in nailing Schultz. He pledged his full support for the mayor's crackdown on the Dutchman.

The Secretary told Hoover much the same thing. Hoover also promised to turn up the heat on Schultz. After his conversation with Morgenthau, the head of the FBI announced that the Dutchman was now an "undercover" Public Enemy Number One. The designation meant the FBI considered Schultz to be one of the top criminals at large in America.

Schultz, who was still officially in hiding, was getting annoyed with all this attention. He wanted to get back to running his rackets without any undue interference from the law.

At this point, he finally realized he couldn't keep duck-ing the charges against him. Wise businessman that he was, Schultz had his lawyers travel to Washington, D.C. in an attempt to negotiate a settlement of his income tax prob-lems. Maybe if he paid up, the feds would leave him alone.

The Dutchman's lawyers met with various officials around town. They also passed word to Morgenthau that Schultz would be glad to pay $100,000 to settle his $92,000 tax bill. A bribe was implicit in the offer.

The Secretary of the Treasury wasn't interested. His reply to Schultz's lawyers was stern and devastating. "We don't do business with criminals," snapped Morgenthau in a rebuke that dashed any hope Schultz might have had of avoiding trial for tax evasion.

Shocked by this response, Schultz made a momentous decision: he would surrender to authorities and take his chances in court. With a bit of luck — and a few bribes — he might be able to beat the rap.

On November 28, 1934, Schultz came out of hiding. He walked warily into the office of the U.S. Commissioner in Albany, New York, and turned himself in. "I'm Arthur Flegenheimer. I am under indictment in the Southern District of New York. I wish to surrender," he told the startled com-missioner. Schultz's period as a fugitive was over.

The Dutchman's bail was set at $50,000, and then doubled — something that greatly annoyed Schultz's main attorney, Dixie Davis. Davis went to court demanding that his client's bail be reduced. After all, Davis reminded the court, Schultz had never actually been convicted of any violent felonies. "Schultz is not a Dillinger. He is not a Baby Face Nelson," argued Davis, referring to two bank-robbing desperadoes of the day. "He is indicted for failure to pay income taxes. Is this a serious crime to man?"

Davis had a ready explanation for why Schultz hadn't bothered paying income taxes in 1929, 1930, and 1931. According to Davis, the Dutchman had virtually no income during this period. Apparently, Schultz had pauperized himself through his noble efforts at providing drink for the alcohol-parched masses.

The judge didn't buy it. Davis couldn't get the income tax charges dismissed, although he did succeed in having Schultz's bail reduced to $75,000. Nonetheless, Schultz had to serve several weeks in jail before he was sprung. It was the longest stretch he had spent behind bars since his sentence for burglary in his youth.

Schultz was eventually told that he would stand trial in the spring of 1935, in Syracuse, New York. Meanwhile, in New York City, another problem was brewing. A Manhattan grand jury had begun looking into municipal corruption and the local numbers racket. Schultz's name was coming up repeatedly in the investigation.

For the moment, however, Schultz was primarily concerned with his tax troubles. After being bailed out of jail, he decided to throw a press conference in Syracuse to proclaim his innocence. With Dixie Davis at his side, he fielded questions from a small army of reporters. The reporters appreciated the opportunity to quiz the gang lord, but were less than impressed by his appearance.

This was a theme the media liked to harp on. A reporter from *The New York Times* once wrote that Schultz looked like "an ill-dressed vagrant." The same journalist noted that the Dutchman "had a special talent for looking like a perfect example of the unsuccessful man."

If the reporters chuckled over Schultz's sense of style, they laughed out loud when he claimed he'd never met Jimmy Hines in his life. But these same members of the press must have thought their ears were playing tricks on them when the brazen Schultz, backed by his learned lawyer, also denied he was ever a bootlegger. "I'm no beer baron," he said. "I never was a beer baron. That'll all come out at the trial."

Schultz provided a brief autobiographical sketch for the journalists, but he wouldn't discuss his father. When asked, Schultz said that his papa had died. He ended the conference by expressing his disgust at being tagged Public Enemy Number One by J. Edgar Hoover. "I'm no public enemy," he insisted. "I'm a public benefactor."

As if the self-proclaimed public benefactor didn't have enough to deal with at that point, he soon had a new problem. While waiting for his trial, Schultz began to suspect that Jules Martin, the man who had masterminded the restaurant rackets, was stiffing him. The Dutchman believed Martin had stolen a total of $70,000 — money that was badly needed now that he might have to pay back-taxes. Schultz was pretty sure that Martin had embezzled this amount to fund some side businesses of his own.

In March 1935, Schultz ordered Martin to withdraw $21,000 in funds from the Metropolitan Restaurant & Cafeteria Owners Association's bank account. To ensure prompt delivery of this cash, Schultz thoughtfully provided two escorts, in the form of Bo Weinberg and Dixie Davis. Weinberg and Davis escorted Martin on a train trip to Cohoes, New York, where Schultz was currently residing.

Once he got to Cohoes, Martin had a man-to-man chat with Schultz in a hotel room. To loosen Martin's tongue, Schultz made sure there was plenty of booze available. Both men drank heavily as they discussed the matter of the missing money. At first, Martin denied that he had stolen any money. In fact, he seemed offended that Schultz even suggested he had done such a thing.

Seeing that he was getting nowhere with his wily associate, Schultz tried a more direct negotiating tactic. He reached over and punched Martin in the face. The trick worked. Stunned, Martin confessed that he had indeed removed some cash from the Restaurant Association's coffers. But he claimed he had taken only $20,000, not $70,000.

If Martin expected mercy from this confession, he was disappointed. Schultz might have studied Catholicism during his time in hiding, but forgiveness was not in his nature.

As his attorney watched in horror, the Dutchman, angry and drunk, snatched an automatic pistol from his belt and slammed the muzzle into Martin's gaping mouth. With a sneer, Schultz pulled the trigger. Martin flew backwards from the impact of the shot. Blood splattered on the small table in front of Schultz as Martin fell to the floor — very dead. "It was as simple and undramatic as that — just one quick motion of the hand," Dixie Davis would later write. "The Dutchman did that murder just as casually as if he were picking his teeth."

Davis was a refined sort — at least in his own mind. He had no problem working with Schultz, but wasn't used to seeing violence so up close and personal. While crime bosses like Al Capone didn't mind getting their hands bloody, Schultz had never been known to commit a murder himself. Davis took Martin's slaying as a sign that the Dutchman was losing control of both his men and his mind.

Schultz's next actions did nothing to allay the attorney's fears. With a look of studied indifference, Schultz began wiping off his bloody gun with a dirty rag. He looked at his lawyer and shrugged. "Sorry you had to see that," he said in an unapologetic tone.

A nervous Davis readily accepted the apology and began discussing the Dutchman's upcoming court case. He tried not to look as Martin's body was removed from the premises.

Davis's firsthand account of Martin's slaying is contradicted by other sources, which state that Bo Weinberg was the real executioner. However, Schultz was fully capable of murder; and as the tides of criminal fortune turned against him, he became more dangerous than ever.

Chapter 7
A Taxing Experience

hen Schultz finally went on trial for tax evasion, few of the prosecution's witnesses were willing to testify. Nearly two dozen of these witnesses took to the hills rather than speak out against the Dutchman. This added an interesting dimension to the trial, which opened on April 16, 1935.

Daniel McCarthy was one of the reluctant witnesses. A former partner of Schultz's from the days when the Dutchman helped run the Hub Social Club, McCarthy showed up at court but never actually testified. While waiting to take the witness stand, he asked it he could go for a walk. Since his presence wasn't required at that immediate moment, legal authorities foolishly allowed him to go. Evidently, they assumed he would come back.

Instead, McCarthy strolled out of the courthouse and vanished. His disappearing act won him a contempt of court charge, but that seemed better than incurring the Dutchman's wrath by testifying.

Such shenanigans did not please the prosecution, which was led by lawyer John McEvers. McEvers was part of the legal team that had convicted Al Capone. He was sure he could nail Schultz as well, if only enough people were brave enough to take the stand.

Those who did speak in court tended to suffer from memory problems or stressed their constitutional right under the Fifth Amendment to remain silent. Bo Weinberg, for example, pleaded the fifth when it came his turn to testify. Other subpoenaed witnesses remained equally tight-lipped.

Among the handful of prosecution witnesses who did testify were Detectives Stephen DiRosa and Julius Salke. These two officers eagerly recounted their early morning encounter with Schultz and the late Danny Iamascia out-side Schultz's apartment four years earlier. The detectives described the brief gunplay that followed this encounter and explained how Schultz offered both of them $50,000 to let him go.

The detectives' testimony was crucial. Essentially, the prosecution was saying that if the Dutchman could throw around $100,000 in bribes, he was clearly making enough money to pay his taxes. So much for Dixie Davis's claim that his client had no income to speak of in the late 1920s and early 1930s.

The prosecution also heard from bankers who testified that Schultz had deposited enormous sums in their vaults, though often under different names. Apparently, 18 banks had handled Schultz's cash during his heyday as Beer Baron of the Bronx.

Schultz's defense took barely three hours, largely because only three witnesses were called. The trio consisted of two lawyers and an accountant who had worked for Schultz. Shamefaced, these mouthpieces said that Schultz was the victim of their lousy legal advice. One by one they confessed that they had inadvertently misled their boss by telling him he didn't have to pay taxes on his illicit income. All three earnestly explained that they had scrambled to make amends as soon as they'd discovered their error, and went on to describe fruitless trips to Washington, D.C. in which they searched for someone willing to accept the Dutchman's back taxes. They rounded out their act by claiming that bureaucratic pettiness was the only thing preventing Schultz from paying what he owed Uncle Sam.

Not to be outdone by his minions, Schultz expanded on this theme when he spoke to reporters outside the courtroom. "I offered $100,000 when the government was broke and people were talking revolution, and they turned me down cold," he said. "You can see now that at least I was willing to pay. Everybody knows that I am being persecuted in this case. I wanted to pay. They were taking it from everybody else but they wouldn't take it from me. I tried to do my duty as a citizen."

In addition to presenting himself as a law-abiding citizen trying to do right, Schultz benefited from the setting of the trial — New York. This was a "wet" state that had rejected Prohibition even before repeal, so New York State residents were less likely than their counterparts in "dry" states to view bootlegging as a serious crime.

Another lucky break came in the nature of the charges against him. Right before the trial began, seven of the counts against Schultz were severed (detached from the list of offenses he faced at trial so they could be used in a separate case). This severance reduced the maximum penalty he faced in Syracuse from 43 years to 16. However, it meant that authorities would have additional tax charges to hold over Schultz's head, should he manage to beat the rap at his current trial. At the time, Schultz didn't see it that way; he was just glad to be facing fewer criminal charges in court.

On April 27, the jury began deliberating. The Dutchman could be seen pacing anxiously up and down the courthouse corridors, chain-smoking during the two days it took the jury to try to reach a decision.

By this point, Schultz's tax travails had become front-page news, and the press was comparing him to Al Capone. Rather than fearing the glare of public scrutiny, Schultz was starting to enjoy the publicity. It took his mind off the fact that he might have to serve a long sentence for tax evasion.

Also, he enjoyed playing the role of big shot gangster for the national media.

Much to Schultz's relief, the trial ended with a hung jury — that is, the jurors couldn't reach a verdict. The justice in the case, Federal Judge Frederick Bryant, had no choice but to discharge the jury and dismiss the court.

"This tough world ain't no place for dunces," exclaimed an exultant Schultz to reporters. "And you can tell those smart guys in New York that the Dutchman is no dunce and as far as he is concerned Alcatraz doesn't exist. I'll never see Alcatraz. Al Capone was a dunce for going to Alcatraz."

Without a trace of irony in his voice, Schultz continued his soliloquy. "I'm no gorilla. I never killed anybody or caused anybody to get killed. They say I was a Beer Baron. Well, what if I was? We got repeal, haven't we? I get a laugh out of anybody calling anybody who gave the people a beer a public enemy. If that is the case, how about Roosevelt?"

Schultz was smart enough not to be overconfident. As the Dutchman and his legal advisors knew, the law was not finished with them yet. Because the Syracuse jury hadn't issued a verdict, authorities were free to order a retrial, which they did almost immediately after Schultz waltzed out of court. The new trial was scheduled to take place in mid-summer in Malone, New York, a small community located near the Canadian border.

While all this was going on, Schultz faced trouble on another front. Throughout the spring of 1935, the grand jury investigating the New York numbers racket had been inundated with evidence of Schultz's illicit activities.

Just when it looked as though the Dutchman would face a fresh indictment, the assistant DA who had been handling the case was abruptly removed. None other than the district attorney himself, Mr. William C. Dodge, replaced him.

Dodge, the man Jimmy Hines had recommended to Schultz as an amiable dunce, soon proved his worth to the gangster. Once he took over the grand jury investigation, the probe into the numbers racket all but ground to a halt.

Dodge had good reason to go slowly. As part of its investigation, the grand jury was beginning to look into connections between the district attorney and Dutch Schultz. The jury was eager to find out if Schultz had funded Dodge's election campaign. Naturally, Dodge didn't want any light thrown on this touchy subject.

The grand jury, however, proved to be tougher than Dodge had expected. They bridled at his control and demanded that he be replaced. In legal parlance, the jurors became "a runaway jury." These runaways wanted the governor of New York, Herbert Lehman, to appoint a special prosecutor to delve into the numbers racket and, presumably, to nail Dutch Schultz.

In June 1935, Governor Lehman bowed to the grand jury's will and appointed Thomas Dewey as a special prosecutor. Schultz's puppet, William Dodge, was infuriated at being pushed aside. It didn't matter; the runaway jury was now looking forward to seeing justice done. Dewey soon began a methodical investigation of the Dutchman's involvement in the numbers racket.

Schultz was justifiably nervous about what the dedicated Dewey would find but figured it would take the lawyer some time to put together a case. In the meantime, he planned to enjoy his freedom and prepare for his second tax trial.

The location of this second trial wasn't reassuring. Malone was a small, conservative town. It might be thought that the inhabitants of such a place would be repulsed by the likes of Dutch Schultz. However, the conniving crook had a plan to win them over.

In early July, several days before the second trial began, Schultz and some of his crew cruised into bucolic Malone. Schultz immediately began throwing money around town, picking up bar and restaurant tabs and doing his best to ingratiate himself with the locals. The Dutchman went to a local baseball game with the mayor and made sure he was friendly and polite to every townsperson he encountered.

For once, Schultz's terrible fashion style played in his favor; Malone residents took one look at his cheap overcoats and threadbare suits and took him to be an average guy — the kind of fellow who didn't try to impress by dressing in a flashy style. He looked more like a hard-working small-town businessman than a high-ranking New York City Mob boss.

Some residents were not impressed by Schultz's presence. Reverend John Williams of the town's First Congregational Church was one. He blasted the Dutchman in a sermon: "I have heard that men in high places will fawn over a gangster and hail his advent because it will bring money to the community," he railed.

Judge Bryant — who was again sitting in the justice's seat — was even less impressed. He revoked Schultz's bail and put him back in jail to prevent him from socializing.

The Dutchman's down-home shtick continued in the courtroom. His team deliberately chose a local attorney as one of their main lawyers in the case. It was a nice touch — the jury, naturally, would be sympathetic to the efforts of a homeboy.

The prosecution offered basically the same case it had presented in Syracuse. Bo Weinberg once more took the stand and pleaded the fifth while other witnesses vanished. Daniel McCarthy was still nowhere to be found.

Schultz again portrayed himself as the victim of bad legal advice. His mouthpieces repeated the sad saga of how they had tried to square away their boss's tax bill, only to be rebuffed at every turn.

It was a clever position to take. The small-town citizens of Malone could sympathize with the notion of a misguided individual being persecuted over his taxes by tyrannical federal authorities. In a struggle with big government, Malone residents could be counted on to root for the little guy.

Schultz's aggressive schmoozing paid off nicely when it came time for the jury to deliberate. On August 1, they voted nine to three for acquittal. Because the judge required a 12–0 vote in order to convict or acquit, he ordered the jury to deliberate further. The next day, the jury voted again and pronounced Schultz "not guilty."

Pandemonium broke out in the courtroom as Schultz's supporters whooped it up. But most of the citizens gasped in shock. Reporters raced to find phones to relay the verdict to their editors.

Schultz was genuinely surprised at his victory. He had launched his charm offensive as a last-ditch attempt to stave off a prison term. He didn't expect to get off scot-free twice in a row.

Judge Bryant was infuriated by both the verdict and the subsequent outburst in the courtroom. He slammed his gavel and brought the courtroom to order. The noise and cheers subsided. Then the justice faced the jurors and gave them a tongue-lashing.

"You have labored long and no doubt have given careful consideration to this case," he said. "Before I discharge you, I will have to say that your verdict is such that it shakes the confidence of law-abiding people in integrity and truth. It will be apparent to all who have followed the evidence in this case that you reached a verdict based not on the evidence, but on some other reason. You will have to go home with the satisfaction, if it is a satisfaction, that you have rendered a blow against law enforcement and given aid and encouragement to people who would flout the law. In all probability, they will commend you. I cannot."

In comments to reporters, jury foreman Leon Chapin disagreed vigorously with the judge's analysis, saying, "We feel that the government just didn't prove its income tax evasion charge. We feel the government utterly failed to show that he earned so much as a nickel of tax income and we based our verdict on that belief. If the government had shown us only $5,000 gross income, we would have convicted."

Back in New York City, Mayor LaGuardia expressed disgust at the verdict. He made it clear to journalists that Schultz was not welcome in his town. "He won't be a resident of New York City," snapped the Little Flower. "We have no place for him here."

When told of this remark by reporters, Schultz couldn't help but gloat. "Tell LaGuardia I will be home tomorrow," he smirked.

Schultz didn't go home to New York, however. He knew authorities hadn't given up trying to put him behind bars. The counts that had been severed from the Syracuse trial could still be used against him. Technically, Dutch Schultz was still a fugitive. There was another reason why Schultz was hesitant to return to his humble abode: the state of New York had gotten into the "get-the-Dutchman" game. New York officials claimed that Schultz owed $36,000 in unpaid taxes to the state. With all this pressure, and LaGuardia and Dewey breathing down his neck, it would be tempting fate to return to Manhattan.

Instead, the Dutchman retreated to Connecticut, where he took up residence in the Stratfield Hotel in Bridgeport. His bodyguard, Bernard "Lulu" Rosenkrantz, accompanied him on his journey.

So engrossed was Schultz with various business affairs that he didn't even bother visiting his girlfriend, who had just given birth to their son, John David. Apparently, fatherhood had lost its charm. Frances looked after John and his sister in a small apartment in Queens. They weren't exactly living large; the Dutchman was as cheap with his family as he was with his wardrobe.

If he wasn't good in the financial aid department, Schultz must have made up for it in other ways. Frances remained charmed by her man and stood by him, even when he kept his distance.

In Connecticut, Schultz did his best to take care of his businesses, which had been neglected during his two trials. He met with Democratic Party boss Jimmy Hines to discuss political and financial issues. The Dutchman informed Hines that due to his legal woes, he would have to cut the party leader's bribes by 50 percent. Schultz talked vaguely of restoring Hines's payoffs to their old level once his legal bills were taken care of.

When not cooking up business deals, the Dutchman found himself the toast of Bridgeport. The local high society thought it was rich and daring to invite Schultz and Rosenkrantz to their parties. The presence of such an infamous gangster apparently added a delicious frisson to society affairs. For the first time in his life, Schultz found himself the center of attention among the yacht club crowd.

Just as the Dutchman had charmed the hicks of Malone, he proved to be gracious and witty at the high-society shindigs he attended in Connecticut. Rosenkrantz accompanied him to some of these events, and apparently he too was quite debonair.

The Dutchman enjoyed the diversion; he had a lot on his mind. Dewey was investigating him, his legal bills were adding up, and his various enterprises had suffered from lack of attention. Other gangsters were already circling, hungrily eyeing his impressive assets. Expecting him to lose the Malone court case, they had been ready to move in and gobble up whatever morsels they fancied.

Bo Weinberg, Schultz's right-hand man, had been certain his boss would be convicted. He had risen high in Schultz's organization and was worried that his position — and all the money and power that went with it — was in jeopardy. Without a steady hand on the tiller, Weinberg was convinced the Schultz empire would collapse. Like Vincent Coll, Weinberg entertained delusions of controlling a slice of the Dutchman's business. The longtime loyal hood turned traitor.

According to some sources, Weinberg approached

Abner "Longy" Zwillman, a top New Jersey mobster. He told Zwillman that Schultz was teetering and explained how other mobsters might benefit from the Dutchman's fall. Zwillman listened, then arranged a meeting with Lucky Luciano.

Other accounts state that Luciano was the player who put the ball into play. According to this version, Luciano had long coveted the Dutchman's criminal empire, so he contacted Weinberg to get the lowdown. Regardless of who first made the invitation, Luciano, Weinberg, and Zwillman had lots to talk about.

Weinberg said he would reveal information on Schultz's criminal empire that would allow Luciano to move in and take it over. In exchange, Weinberg wanted a healthy cut of any future action. Luciano mulled over Weinberg's proposal, then arranged a meeting at his Waldorf Towers apartment.

Some of the biggest mobsters in the country attended this tête-à-tête, including Joe Adonis, Frank Costello, Meyer Lansky, Louis "Lepke" Buchalter, Thomas Lucchese, and Vito Genovese. These men represented the inner circle of the Commission — the national criminal organization Luciano had put together. They were the crème de la crime, so to speak.

At the meeting, Luciano outlined Weinberg's deal. In spite of Schultz's impressive winning streak in court, the gangsters assumed that the government would eventually nail him. After all, the feds had managed to get Al Capone behind bars, and he was a considerably bigger fish than

Dutch Schultz. Luciano proposed to divide Schultz's empire between members of the inner circle, with everyone getting a fair share.

If Schultz knew about this plotting and scheming, he didn't let on. He did find out about Bo Weinberg's betrayal eventually, however. The Dutchman was furious — and hurt. Weinberg was one of his most trusted goons. How dare he defect after all these years?

Livid, Schultz decided that Weinberg had to die. As he had proven with Mad Dog Coll, the Dutchman had little patience for ungrateful employees. When Schultz learned that Weinberg was meeting regularly with Longy Zwillman at the Zwillman mansion, he ordered his crew to stake out the palatial estate. Sure enough, they soon noted Weinberg coming and going.

On September 9, 1935, Schultz had Weinberg picked up as he left Zwillman's. The traitor was taken for a one-way ride. During the days that followed Bo Weinberg's disappearance, there emerged several colorful gangland tales that detailed what had happened to Bo.

One version had it that Schultz killed his old lieutenant with his bare hands. Another story claimed that the Dutchman merely beat him almost senseless, then ordered his goons to coat Weinberg's feet with cement and dump him into the East River — while he was still alive. The ride to the river must have given Weinberg lots of time to regret turning on his old boss.

A Taxing Experience

The move to take over the Dutchman's criminal empire was put on hold — at least for the time being.

Chapter 8
Dewey v. the Dutchman

Two weeks after getting rid of Bo Weinberg, Schultz moved from Bridgeport, Connecticut, to Perth Amboy, New Jersey. The Dutchman still hadn't made good on his vow to return to New York City.

While Schultz had been acquitted in Malone, he wasn't off the hook just yet. The feds held a warrant against him for the tax charges that had been severed in Syracuse. Plus, the state of New York was after Schultz for $36,000 in unpaid taxes. Until he settled these matters, Schultz was technically still a fugitive in the eyes of the law.

Schultz tried to keep a low profile in Perth Amboy. He registered at the Packer Hotel as Morris Golden and did his best to stay under the radar. However, he was too well known at this point to evade the careful scrutiny of the public. Just as a nosy neighbor had blown his cover at the fancy apartment in New York, someone in Perth Amboy gave Schultz away.

The police duly showed up. They checked in on Mr. Golden and discovered he was indeed the notorious Dutchman. Schultz surrendered without a fight. The cops took him down to the station and charged him with "suspicion of being a fugitive."

Shortly after Schultz was bailed out, government lawyers secured a bench warrant against him, demanding his re-arrest on untried tax charges. Schultz's attorneys rushed back into court to defend their man's honor. A judicial brouhaha erupted as Dixie Davis and other Schultz lawyers argued with government prosecutors. Davis claimed that his client was being "persecuted" by state authorities — which wasn't too far off the mark. Meanwhile, Schultz was put back in jail. Bailed out again, on October 1, Schultz had some nasty things to say about his pursuers. "The federal government is hounding me," he snapped to a flock of reporters. "They tried me on the same charge in New York and now they dug up a new trick to repeat the maneuver."

Again, this wasn't just gangster paranoia. Authorities were still determined to nail Schultz for being a delinquent taxpayer. Considering Schultz had already won two court battles over this matter, the state was showing remarkable resolve.

Disillusioned with the charms of Perth Amboy, Schultz

moved to Newark, New Jersey, where he set up shop at the Robert Treat Hotel. It was still too hot to step foot in New York State, much less Manhattan.

This time, Schultz didn't register under a phony name or attempt to keep out of the spotlight. Quite the contrary; he decided it was time to launch a new "charm" offensive. The cunning crook figured that a dose of public sympathy might ease his latest tax problems. Perhaps if he wooed the locals, potential jurors might look at him with sympathetic eyes, just as they had in Malone.

Schultz selected a local restaurant called the Palace Chop House as his temporary headquarters. A former speak-easy, the Chop House served decent food and was located near his hotel. The restaurant featured a 60-foot bar, eight booths, and an assortment of tables in a back room. The low-key ambience of the place met the Dutchman's approval.

With his bodyguards Lulu Rosenkrantz and Abe Landau by his side, Schultz patronized the Palace Chop House almost every night for supper. During mealtime he issued orders to various minions, listened to reports from the field, and discussed future plans with his flunkies. He also held court for a stream of reporters and interested locals.

In an interview with the Newark *Star Ledger*, the Dutchman tried to pose as a man more sinned against than sinned. When asked about the federal government's latest charges against him, Schultz bristled. "They're after me now because some puny individuals in the government services can't stand up and take a licking like a man," he scoffed. "By licking I mean they can't swallow that I was acquitted once and another jury disagreed on exactly the same charges they've got against me now."

Striking a tone of deep hurt, the Dutchman said that the government had used "perjured witnesses" in both his tax trials. He managed to sound outraged over this dubious affront.

Perhaps Schultz was getting cocky, having beaten the federal government twice in court. Or perhaps he was beginning to believe his own PR. He also told the Newark *Star Ledger* reporter that he was through with crime — a statement that had to rank as one of Schultz's biggest whoppers. Crime had made Dutch Schultz rich and it was the only thing he was really good at. He compounded this falsehood by indicating that he wanted to become an average Joe. "I want to settle down and be a plain citizen and be given a chance to earn a living," stated the Dutchman. "I want to be plain Arthur Flegenheimer and forget there ever was a Dutch Schultz."

Unfortunately for Flegenheimer, the feds would not let him forget his other identity. On October 9, 1935, a federal grand jury formalized the untried tax charges against him. The jury couldn't indict Schultz for felony tax evasion, as this would constitute double jeopardy (being charged twice for the same offense). To avoid this trap, the grand jury hit Schultz with a bunch of lesser counts that hadn't been used in his previous trials. Schultz was indicted on misdemeanor charges for failing to file income tax returns in 1929, 1930, and 1931.

While Thomas Dewey was hardly the only lawyer on the Dutchman's case, Schultz was rapidly becoming fixated on him in particular. Schultz began to view the special prosecutor as his nemesis.

During the fall, Schultz launched a private war against Dewey. The prosecutor's heavily pregnant wife — who was also named Frances — started to get menacing phone calls. Whether the caller in question was Schultz or one of his goons is unclear. At any rate, Frances Dewey was terrified. The unidentified caller issued vague threats that kept her on edge. On one occasion, she was informed her husband was dead and that she was required to identify his corpse.

Meanwhile, Dewey heard a rumor that there was a $25,000 bounty on his head, payable by Dutch Schultz. While hoods made threats against government prosecutors all the time, they rarely carried through with them. In this case, though, authorities took the rumors seriously. Dewey was soon assigned a pair of bodyguards.

The FBI's J. Edgar Hoover also got in on the act. He sent Dewey a letter urging him to be cautious. Hoover, too, had heard rumors that Schultz was plotting Dewey's demise. He knew it was do or die with the Dutchman.

On October 18, a newspaper called the *Philadelphia Evening Bulletin* published a profile entitled "Dutch Schultz Weeps In His Jello for Gang Widows and Orphans." The author of the piece had interviewed Schultz mid-meal, and Schultz had offered the man some jello in between bites of his dessert. The article was a rehash of Schultz's usual gripes against the government, but also included a conspiracy theory à la Dutch. "It's always a good popular play for the government to go after the racketeers," said Schultz. "It keeps folks' minds off bank closings and widows and orphans being swindled."

This was an interesting — albeit hypocritical — tangent. After all, Schultz was working hard to make an orphan of Dewey's unborn baby. To achieve this vicious end, Schultz petitioned the Commission to okay a hit on the prosecutor. To kill a high-ranking government official such as Thomas Dewey, Schultz needed to get permission first.

Largely a regulatory body, concerned with rules and maintaining order, the Commission had a proactive arm. When its existence came to light, the media dubbed this arm "Murder, Incorporated."

Murder, Inc. consisted of a bunch of dedicated killers on permanent retainer. The Commission would order a hit, and Murder, Inc. would carry it out. According to some accounts, Murder, Inc. was responsible for 500 to 700 deaths during the 1930s. Many of these killings were of errant gangsters who had crossed the Commission or made a fatal breech of gangster etiquette.

The sociopaths in Murder, Inc. were usually content to shoot their victims. When the situation required it, however, they were also capable of faking accidents and staging suicides. An all-around bunch of professionals, the Murder, Inc. crew represented the gold standard for hit men. As far as Schultz was concerned, they were the perfect bunch to bump off Dewey.

There was a snag, however. The Commission frowned on killing cops, lawyers, judges, and politicians. The reason was more pragmatic than pacifistic. Murdering a ranking legal authority would generate a huge amount of negative publicity. The public and press would be outraged and the forces of law and order would seek revenge. Though the Commission's code of ethics might have been a bit twisted, its members followed it nonetheless. Schultz was raising hackles by threatening to violate this code.

There are several variations on what happened next. In the most commonly told version, Lucky Luciano called an emergency meeting of the Commission to discuss Schultz's idea. The Dutchman snuck into the city just to attend this meeting. He had finally made it back to New York, albeit under less than triumphant circumstances.

It must have been a strained meeting. The top gangsters were no doubt disappointed that Dutch Schultz had beaten the charges against him. His acquittal meant they couldn't seize his empire. There was also the matter of Bo Weinberg's betrayal. It's not certain if Schultz knew that Luciano had been in cahoots with Weinberg, but he must have suspected such a collusion. However, Dutch kept his suspicions to himself and concentrated on the matter of Dewey.

During the meeting, Schultz forcibly made the case for Dewey's demise. The mobsters in attendance listened to him, then began debating whether the prosecutor should be stopped.

Killing someone of Dewey's stature was not the kind of assignment that could be done in a hurry, noted the crime bosses. To Schultz's annoyance, the gangsters decided to wait a week before making a decision on the proposed assassination. In the meantime, a hit man would be assigned to determine how Dewey could be killed — should it be so ordered.

The hit man tapped for this task was Albert Anastasia, aka "the Mad Hatter" or "Lord High Executioner of Murder, Inc." He was a devoted professional and the perfect thug to arrange a hit on a well-protected prosecutor.

Anastasia had begun his criminal career on the docks in Brooklyn, working as an enforcer for a mobster-controlled longshoreman's union. His talent for mayhem soon got noticed, and he became a hired assassin for Murder, Inc. The Mad Hatter had a bloodlust that rivaled that of Vincent "Mad Dog" Coll. His resume was filled with important hits.

Anastasia might have been a vicious thug, but he was also a careful planner. He decided to stake out his quarry. To pull this off, Anastasia needed some cover. A small boy was procured — probably the son of a fellow mobster — along with a tricycle.

Equipped with kid and trike, the Mad Hatter began

spending his mornings outside Dewey's apartment. The boy
would ride about on the sidewalk while the hit man pretend-
ed to watch him. Anyone walking by would assume Anastasia
was a devoted family man spending quality time with his son
before going to work. Certainly Dewey never noticed the boy
on his bike. The special prosecutor seemed oblivious to the
fact that one of Murder, Inc.'s top-ranked killers was lingering
around his doorstep.

Anastasia and the young boy made an appearance four
mornings in a row. Through this subterfuge, the Mad Hatter
was able to get a pretty good sense of Dewey's daily routine.
Typically, the prosecutor left his house each morning around
8 a.m. in the presence of his two newly assigned bodyguards.
The three men would journey a couple of blocks to a nearby
drugstore, where Dewey always stopped before going to his
office. The bodyguards would stand outside while the special
prosecutor called his office from the pharmacy's pay phone.

Dewey would later claim that he made calls from the
drugstore so as not to disturb his wife back home. This seemed
pretty unlikely. A more plausible reason was that Dewey was
probably worried that his home phone was tapped.

Anastasia soon came to the conclusion that the drugstore would be the perfect place to kill Dewey. With the
location squared away, he finished his preparations for the
possible hit. Selecting an impressive array of guns, he gouged
out the serial numbers to make them untraceable. Then he
adjusted the barrels and attached silencers. Finally, he stole a

vehicle for use as a potential getaway car.

In the second meeting of the Commission, Anastasia described Dewey's daily drugstore ritual and explained how the prosecutor could be killed. Schultz listened carefully as the meticulous assassin told the group he would plant himself in the pharmacy a few minutes before Dewey arrived and buy something to allay the suspicions of the pharmacist. If all went to plan, Dewey would arrive at the pharmacy at his usual time and go straight to the phone booth. At this point, Anastasia would draw his carefully concealed weapon and plug him. Dewey would be a sitting duck inside the booth — just as Vincent Coll had been. Thanks to the silencer, the bodyguards outside the drugstore wouldn't hear any shots. They would be watching the street, keeping their eyes peeled for anyone trying to follow the prosecutor.

After Dewey was dead, Anastasia would kill the pharmacy owner and anyone else unlucky enough to be inside the drugstore. Having disposed of any potential witnesses, the shooter would put away his piece and stroll outside. He would saunter past the two bodyguards and make his way to the getaway car parked conveniently around a corner. Anastasia would tear away from the scene, then ditch both the car and his gun.

The members of the Commission listened to this plan with interest. The general feeling was that a hit on Dewey was "doable." But whether it was wise was another matter.

The gangsters began to debate the pros and cons of

killing the prosecutor. Schultz's fury mounted as members of the Commission raised strong opposition to hitting Dewey. Lepke Buchalter was vehemently against the hit. He pointed out that if Dewey were to be killed, authorities would crack down on Mob activity across the nation. It wasn't even necessary to kill Dewey to stop his investigation, Buchalter continued. All the Commission had to do was find out what witnesses Dewey had lined up and kill them before they could testify. This seemed a far safer option than gunning down the special prosecutor himself.

Lucky Luciano seconded Lepke's objections, and added a few of his own. The general consensus among the mobsters was that killing Dewey would be more trouble than it was worth.

Schultz had heard enough. Throwing every shred of caution to the wind, he leapt out of his chair and announced that if the Commission wouldn't sanction the hit, he would do it himself. The other gangsters looked at each other in alarm as the enraged Schultz stormed out. Was this crazy guy serious?

Schultz's behavior following the meeting indicated that he was. As a rule, Mob hits were conducted under a veil of secrecy and silence — too much talk might alert the victim and spoil the hit. The Dutchman ignored this golden rule and boasted to everyone within earshot that he was going to kill Thomas Dewey. He seemed to relish the notion of performing the deed himself.

Dewey v. the Dutchman

The Commission was not amused. The members wondered if Schultz's delicate mental equilibrium had become completely unbalanced. Suppose police arrested Schultz before he could pull off the hit. The Dutchman might snap under interrogation and spill the beans about his comrades in crime. He was rarely in full control of his faculties these days, even in the best of times.

There was one final consideration on the table: for all his legal problems, the Dutchman's business domain was still relatively healthy and profitable. The Commission had already mentally divided up Schultz's spoils among themselves when they thought Bo Weinberg was going to take him out. It would seem a shame not to carry through with the plans.

Luciano led his criminal compatriots in another high-level policy session to decide Schultz's fate. It didn't take long to reach a decision. The Dutchman had to die.

Chapter 9
The Chop House Massacre

October 23, 1935, was unusually warm for fall. At around 6 p.m. Dutch Schultz, Abe Landau, and Lulu Rosenkrantz stepped into the Palace Chop House in Newark for a working supper. As always, Landau and Rosenkrantz were performing bodyguard duties. Schultz had so much faith in these men that he wasn't even carrying a gun.

The Chop House was empty, except for a couple of regulars tossing back drinks at the bar. The three men strolled the length of the 60-foot bar and stepped into the back room. There, they sat in their usual place — a large round table against a wall. This spot had a strategic advantage. It offered a place where Dutch could sit with his back protected, while keeping an eye on the doorway.

Schultz sat down in his privileged position as his flunkies occupied the other chairs around the table. A waiter came by to take the mens' drink requests and returned shortly with a tray of booze.

If the gangsters liked to dine at the same table, they also tended to select the same meals over and over again. The moment they came in, the chef started preparing an order of steaks and French fries.

A fourth man — Otto "Abbadabba" Berman, the genius fixer of the numbers racket — soon joined Schultz's table. The men soon became so engrossed in their business discussion that they didn't notice when the restaurant's other patrons left.

Meals were served and Schultz and company briefly paused in their fiscal calibrations to eat. Once the greasy plates were cleared away, they went back to work. For all the difficulties he was having keeping his empire together, Schultz was still pulling in thousands of dollars a day from his enterprises.

At 9 p.m., Jacob Friedman, co-owner of the Chop House, arrived to take a shift behind the bar. Noting that the Schultz gang were the only customers, he figured he was in for a quiet evening.

Around 10:15, Friedman was about to drink a cup of coffee when two men came in. He froze. Something about the newcomers unnerved him. They both wore topcoats – unbuttoned — and scowls. Friedman dove for cover. He hit the floor behind the bar as the two intruders, Charlie "the Bug" Workman and Emmanuel "Mendy" Weiss, made their way to the back room. They knew where to find their quarry.

The two men were both on Lepke Buchalter's payroll, and they were keen to get on with their evening's work. Underneath his coat, Workman had a .38 caliber revolver and a .45 automatic pistol. Weiss had a double-barreled shotgun. There were only three men at the table when the thugs peered in — the Dutchman's chair was empty. Workman, figuring the fourth man was in the washroom, signaled Weiss to keep the trio covered. They were still so engrossed in their work that they didn't realize they were being watched.

Workman stormed into the washroom with his .45 drawn and blasted the sole occupant. The hit man couldn't see his target's face because he had his back to the door, so he wasn't sure if he had hit Schultz or one of his cronies. Without identifying the wounded man sprawled on the floor, he tore out of the john and ran back into the dining area.

Hearing the shots, Schultz's associates sprang into action. Landau and Rosenkrantz tried to draw their own pieces while the unarmed Berman just stared, bug-eyed in horror. Weiss squeezed both triggers of his shotgun and sprayed the men with a barrage of bullets. In the confined quarters of the back room, the discharge sounded like a nuclear detonation.

Ears ringing from the shotgun blast, Workman also rushed at the table, shooting in rapid-fire fashion. He swiveled his gun from target to target, blasting away like an Old West gunfighter. One by one, the three men sprawled backwards, splattering blood over the pile of financial sheets as they fell.

The men were hit numerous times and were badly wounded but, amazingly, they were still alive. Looking at their bloodied faces, Workman realized the man in the washroom had indeed been Schultz. Leaving Weiss to guard the others, he rushed back to the john.

There, he found Schultz, half-lying, half-sitting, his eyes wide and vacant. The bullet had entered his body on the left side and torn into his abdomen. The round passed through his large intestine, gall bladder, and liver. The Dutchman's spleen and stomach were perforated as well. He gripped his wound and didn't even turn his head as Workman slammed back into the washroom. But for some unknown reason, Workman didn't finish the job. Instead, as Weiss later surmised, he rifled through Schultz's pockets, looking for cash.

Meanwhile, Weiss was getting nervous because his partner was taking so long. Taking matters into his own hands, he turned on his heels and fled the Chop House. He jumped into a running getaway car where a third hit man, known only as Piggy, sat behind the wheel. With a grunt from Weiss, Piggy gunned the motor and raced away. A more intelligent gunman might have made sure his victims were dead before taking off.

Back in the Chop House, Landau had regained his senses and was struggling to stand up. He was determined to get back at the gunmen. Staring around the room with wild eyes, he drew his gun.

At this point, Workman came rushing back out of the men's room. Astonished to see Landau lurching about, trying to draw a bead on him — and realizing that his cohort had taken off — the infuriated Workman dashed out of the restaurant. Cursing loudly, he ran as fast as he could.

By this time, Landau had also reached the street and was doing his best to put a few bullets into Workman's back. The horribly wounded gangster waved his pistol in Workman's general direction and started firing. Landau's aim was more than a little off and his rounds hit everything but Workman. Bullets ricocheted off the sides of buildings and threatened the lives of passers-by.

Landau kept firing until his clip was empty. In no shape to reload, he did a mad little dance on the sidewalk. Then his knees buckled. To steady himself, Landau sat down on a garbage can. His unloaded pistol clattered to the ground. He remained seated on the trashcan, looking as though he was part of the day's rubbish. The picture would have been amusing, but for the trail of blood on the sidewalk.

While this drama unfolded outside, the Dutchman struggled to his feet and wobbled out of the men's room. With his mouth contorted into an agonized grimace, the white-faced Schultz lurched forward, leaking blood. He moved with the stiff-legged grace of Frankenstein's monster. Rosenkrantz, who was just recovering, looked on with awe, amazed that his boss was still alive. Berman, who was still out of it, didn't even notice that Schultz had entered the room.

Mumbling that he needed a doctor, the Dutchman sat down hard in a chair. Onlookers might have taken Schultz for a drunk trying to steady himself — until they noticed the blood.

Once seated, Schultz fell face first against a table, hands splayed by the sides of his head as if he were diving into a swimming pool. A subsequent photo of him in this pose became a gangster classic.

Perhaps inspired by Schultz's example, Rosenkrantz slowly got up. He walked, very unsteadily, to the bar. Placing his hands on the counter for support, Rosenkrantz demanded change to make a phone call. The shaken Friedman, who had wisely remained hidden behind the bar, stood up and immediately gave the bodyguard a nickel. With trembling fingers, the bodyguard dialed zero and croaked into the receiver. He had called the police.

This was probably the first time in years that anyone in Schultz's gang had contacted the cops for help. Not that Rosenkrantz had many alternatives — there were few fellow gangsters he could call for assistance.

As it turned out, the police and ambulance staffers were already on their way. The gunplay had attracted the attention of concerned citizens. Newark was not New York; barroom shoot-outs were not the norm in this city.

Once the authorities arrived, the wounded men received

some basic first-aid to stem their bleeding. Police asked the Dutchman if he were indeed Dutch Schultz. He responded in the affirmative, but — as expected — wouldn't say who shot him. The four hoods were then rushed to Newark City Hospital and placed under tight guard. The cops were determined not to let Schultz's enemies finish the job.

Something else concerned the police. They knew that if the quartet were to die, the Chop House ambush would be the biggest gangster mass execution since the St. Valentine's Day Massacre in Chicago. This was not the kind of publicity Newark wanted.

True to the gangsters' code, the criminal foursome remained silent on any questions of importance. Schultz again denied knowing who shot him and demanded that the cops leave him alone. Rosenkrantz roared at the men in blue to get him an ice cream soda.

While doctors in Newark worked frantically to save the four men's lives, the purge of Schultz's organization continued. Other anti-Schultz gangsters turned their attention to Marty Krompier in New York City. Krompier was the buddy who had backed Schultz in the Club Abbey brawl back in 1931. He was now a lieutenant in the Schultz organization and had been managing the New York enterprises while the boss was in exile from the Big Apple.

Krompier was in the habit of making an evening stop at the Hollywood Barber Shop at 7th Avenue and 47th Street in New York. He liked to get a late-night shave before hitting the town. Shortly after Schultz and his associates had been gunned down at the Palace Chop House, a pair of assassins paid Krompier a visit. The two blasted him in the barbershop, but proved to be as sloppy as Workman and Weiss.

Badly wounded but still breathing, Krompier was taken by ambulance to New York's Polyclinic Hospital — the same place where Arnold Rothstein had died after being shot seven years earlier. Like Schultz, Krompier was still alive, but barely.

While Krompier was treated at the Polyclinic Hospital, doctors in Newark operated on the Dutchman. There wasn't much they could do. Schultz had endured massive internal damage and bleeding. Peritonitis (swelling of the abdomen wall) had set in. Penicillin was unknown at the time, making such a condition life threatening.

After surgery, Schultz was placed in a small room under heavy police guard. Subsequent photographs showed him on his back, naked torso exposed, a look of shock and disbelief on his face.

Aware that his chances for survival were slim, Schultz asked for a priest. The Dutchman wanted to convert to Catholicism before it was too late. One Father Cornelius McInerney arrived and Schultz was baptized and given the last rites of the Catholic Church.

The Dutchman's flunkies were not in any better shape. Abbadabba Berman went first, expiring at 2:55 a.m. on the morning of October 24. A few hours later, Landau, who had lost huge amounts of blood at the scene of the shooting, also died.

News of the Palace Chop House massacre spread quickly through the underworld. Members of the Commission were pleased, albeit slightly concerned that Schultz was still alive.

According to legend, Schultz received a telegram at this point, from Stephanie St. Clair — the former Policy Queen of Harlem. The fabled telegram was sent by Western Union and arrived at the reception desk of the hospital. Fittingly, considering Schultz's deathbed conversion, the message contained a religious quote. It read: "As ye sew, so shall ye reap."

Chapter 10
The Fading Star

By late afternoon of October 24, 1935, the physicians treating Dutch Schultz expected him to die at any moment. Peritonitis had caused Schultz's temperature to spike wildly. With his temperature hovering around 106 degrees, the Dutchman began drifting in and out of consciousness. As he faded, he began to babble. He lay on his back, clutching his head in his hands, moaning and offering an eerie monologue.

Meanwhile, photographers crowded into the room and began snapping pictures. The police weren't concerned about Schultz's right to privacy. As a result, his death spasms were recorded in black and white, to be splashed on the front pages of newspapers across the country.

The press weren't the only ones who wanted to preserve

the moment. The police thought this was a golden opportunity to pick up some insider information. They hoped the Dutchman would give away Mob secrets in his deathbed delirium. At 4 p.m., the cops installed a stenographer in Schultz's room, with instructions to take down everything he said. But instead of Mob secrets, the stenographer captured the Dutchman's bizarre death prattle.

For the next two hours, Schultz weaved a mad tapestry of unconnected phrases, jumbled statements, and strange oaths as his mind darted back and forth through the course of his criminal life. As Schultz rambled, his mother, sister, brother-in-law, and girlfriend gathered around his bed and bewailed his fate. This hospital visit was the first time that Schultz's mother met Frances. Considering the circumstances, it's safe to say their initial encounter was not a happy affair.

When questioned by police authorities, Mrs. Flegenheimer insisted she didn't know her son was a gangster. The police concluded that the old woman was either unusually dense or in a strong state of denial — Schultz's antics had been front-page news for years.

After babbling for hours, Schultz entered a final death spiral. At 6 p.m., he spoke his last words: "French-Canadian bean soup! I want to pay. Let them leave me alone."

Frances came into the room and sat by him, but the Dutchman had lapsed into a coma. At 8:35 p.m. on October 24, he died.

Only 33 years old, the nation's leading maverick mobster was gone. Fittingly, Schultz didn't offer any poignant goodbyes to his family or profound epitaphs for future historians. Instead, his final words were as garbled and strange as his adult life had been.

Schultz's individualistic attitude and contrary spirit earned him a fortune, and his offbeat cockiness helped him endure a long campaign of judicial harassment. Most gangsters would have crumpled and begged for a deal, but Schultz defiantly took on the federal government.

However, this attitude and spirit were his downfall as well as his strength. His peers arranged his murder, largely for refusing to submit to the group dictates of a criminal collective.

No one understood what motivated the Dutchman to do some of the strange things he is remembered for, or what made him become so obsessed with killing Thomas Dewey. It was appropriate, then, that no one had a clue what Schultz was talking about as he wailed on his deathbed.

Dutch Schultz was buried on October 28, 1935, at the Gates of Heaven Cemetery in Hawthorne, a small community outside New York City. His family and Father McInerney were the only mourners present at his funeral.

Father McInerney performed a brief Catholic service for the slain mobster. Despite the presence of the good father, the funeral service took on an ecumenical flavor when Emma Flegenheimer draped a Jewish prayer shawl on the coffin.

The absence of Schultz's criminal compatriots high-lighted the Dutchman's low standing with his fellow members at the time of his assassination. In death, as in life, he remained a loner, determined to make his own rules — a loose cannon in the increasingly organized world of crime.

* * *

Lulu Rosenkrantz expired eight hours after Schultz died. He had lived the longest of the four men who had been shot up in the Palace Chop House ambush.

Marty Krompier was the only Schultz associate who didn't die in the purge. He recovered from his injuries and was released from hospital in early 1936.

Thomas Dewey continued to probe Schultz's criminal empire, even after the Dutchman's death. On July 14, 1937, a grand jury indicted Dixie Davis, George Weinberg, and a man named Harry Schoenhaus for their involvement in the Harlem policy rackets. Dewey cut a deal with these three men. They would receive lenient treatment in exchange for testifying against Democratic Party leader Jimmy Hines.

The men testified, and Hines was arrested in the spring of 1938 on corruption charges. He was put on trial in August. A mistrial ensued. Legal authorities wouldn't give up, and in late January 1939, Hines faced a second trial.

At this point, George Weinberg — who was being held under heavy police guard — committed suicide with a pistol belonging to one of his erstwhile protectors.

Dewey used Weinberg's earlier testimony to convict Hines at his second trial. In 1940, the former Democratic Party boss was sentenced to four to eight years in prison. Hines served four years and was released in the fall of 1944. He died in 1957.

Thomas Dewey was elected district attorney for the County of New York in 1937 and governor of New York State in 1943. He served three terms as governor. He ran, unsuccessfully, for president in 1944 and 1948. Dewey remained active in Republican political circles even after these twin defeats. He died in 1971 in Florida, having outlived Dutch Schultz by several decades.

Dixie Davis received only one year in jail, thanks to his role in testifying against Hines. Upon his release, he wrote a sensational account of his life with Dutch Schultz.

On December 31, 1969, Davis discovered that armed burglars had robbed his Bel Air home and tied up his wife, grandson, and maid. On seeing the ransacked house, he had a heart attack and died.

Charles "the Bug" Workman's complaints about being abandoned at the Chop House almost resulted in the execution of Emmanuel "Mendy" Weiss, for dereliction of mobster duty. Weiss avoided death only because his superiors believed his tale of a tardy Workman going through Schultz's pockets.

Workman was fingered for the Schultz killing by Abe

Reles, aka "Kid Twist," a Murder, Inc. gunman. In June 1941, Charlie the Bug was put on trial for killing Schultz and his dining companions. Workman was found guilty and remained in prison until 1964.

Mendy Weiss was never tried for killing Schultz, although he was convicted of an unassociated murder. Along with his boss, Lepke Buchalter, Weiss was electrocuted in the Sing Sing prison electric chair in 1944.

Charles "Lucky" Luciano was incarcerated in 1936 after Thomas Dewey cracked down on his prostitution business. During World War II, Luciano was released from jail after assisting the U.S. federal government. Among other favors, he allegedly provided contacts that proved useful in the Allied invasion of Sicily and Italy. After the war ended, Luciano was deported to Italy, where he died in 1962.

Albert Anastasia graduated from being a hit man to a crime boss. He was shot dead — probably by his fellow gangsters — in the barbershop of the Park Sheraton Hotel in New York City on October 25, 1957.

Frances "Flegenheimer" moved out of New York City and kept a low profile as she raised her two children. Little is known about her subsequent life.

Murder, Inc. began to fall apart in the early 1940s after some of its members, including Abe Reles, were arrested. Reles broke the mobster "code of silence" and told the police about the inner workings of Murder, Inc., the existence of which had only been a rumor until that point.

Reles provided information on an estimated 200 murders that he had either committed or knew about. His confessions led to several arrests. Reles died in police custody in November 1941, after mysteriously falling out of a seven-story window.

The Commission — the national crime syndicate organized by Lucky Luciano and Meyer Lansky — still exists today, albeit in a greatly truncated form. Decades of arrests, trials, and intra-Mob warfare have reduced the Commission to a shell of its former self.

Epilogue

For modern gangsters with a sense of history, the story of Dutch Schultz's astonishing rise and equally fast fall offers a cautionary tale about impulsive behavior, the limits of violence, and the importance of observing Mob etiquette.

The rules of the modern underworld remain the same as they were in Schultz's day: respect your peers, get permission for big hits and, most of all, don't kill anyone who might cause more problems dead than alive.

In the decades since he died, Dutch Schultz has become a pop culture icon. His deeds have been portrayed in films and books, including the movie *Hoodlum*, with Tim Roth as the Dutchman, and the novel *Billy Bathgate* by famed American writer E.L. Doctorow. This book was turned into a movie starring Dustin Hoffman as Schultz.

As remarkable as his criminal life was, Schultz's immortality was really assured by his bizarre deathbed monologue. In 1970, notorious avant-garde author William Burroughs published a book based on Schultz's death prattle. Entitled *The Last Words of Dutch Schultz: A Fiction In the Form of a Film Script*, Burroughs used snippets of the Dutchman's dying words to create a bizarre, hallucinatory text.

Roughly three decades later, composer Eric Salzman unveiled an opera, also entitled *The Last Words of Dutch*

Epilogue

Schultz. As in Burroughs's book, the opera examined Schultz's life, as he lay dying in Newark City Hospital. The Dutch Schultz opera premiered in Amsterdam in 1997.

The Dutchman would have been amused. While many of his contemporaries have vanished from the national consciousness, Schultz's life and dramatic death retain a vivid grip on the public imagination.

Further Reading

Asbury, Herbert. *The Gangs of New York.* New York: Thunder's Mouth Press, 1927.

Behr, Edward. *Prohibition: Thirteen Years That Changed America.* New York: Arcade Publishing, 1996.

De Champlain, Pierre. *Mobsters, Gangsters and Men of Honour.* Toronto: HarperCollins, 2004.

Doctorow, E.L. *Billy Bathgate.* New York: Penguin, 1989.

Kobler, John. *Capone: The Life and World of Al Capone.* Cambridge, MA: Da Capo Press (a member of the Perseus Books Group), 1971.

Lacey, Robert. *Little Man: Meyer Lansky and the Gangster Life.* Boston: Little, Brown and Company, 1991.

Mannion, James. *The Everything Mafia Book.* Avon, MA: Adams Media Corporation, 2003.

Reppetto, Thomas. *American Mafia: A History of Its Rise to Power.* New York: Henry Holt and Company, 2004.

Sann, Paul. *Kill the Dutchman! The Story of Dutch Schultz.* New Rochelle, NY: Arlington House, 1971.

Smith, Jo Durden. *Mafia: The Complete History of a Criminal World.* London: Arcturus Publishing, 2003.

Turkus, Burton and Sid Feder. *Murder, Inc. The Story of the Syndicate.* Cambridge, MA: Da Capo Press, 1951.

Zion, Sidney. *Loyalty and Betrayal: The Story of the American Mob.* San Francisco: Collins Publishers, 1994.

**Note: A complete transcript of Dutch Schultz's last words was published in the October 26, 1935 edition of *The New York Times*. It was reprinted in Paul Sann's 1971 book, *Kill the Dutchman!*

Dutch Schultz's last words can also be read online at: http://www.killthedutchman.net/

Acknowledgments

Writing is a solitary occupation, but that doesn't mean I was alone when I put this book together. I want to thank the folks at Altitude Publishing for their support and encouragement. Ditto for my girlfriend, Alyson, who was forced to read the rough draft and comment on it numerous times. My parents, Brian and Margaret, were also supportive — if somewhat amused by my current fixation with crime writing.

I would also like to praise the efforts of writers before me whose work was invaluable for my research and understanding of the complex character that was Dutch Schultz. Two books in particular set the gold standard for Schultz-related history: Paul Sann's hardboiled epic, *Kill the Dutchman!*, and the equally gripping *Murder, Inc.*, by Burton Turkus and Sid Feder. If my book holds even a glimmer of the greatness of these two tomes, I will consider I have done a good job. I also wish to acknowledge these two titles and the online www.crimelibrary.com for quotes included in this book.

Photo Credits

Cover: The Library of Congress

About the Author

Nate Hendley is a freelance writer/reporter. He is the author of *Edwin Alonzo Boyd: The Life and Crimes of Canada's Master Bank Robber* and *The Black Donnellys: The Outrageous Tale of Canada's Deadliest Feud,* both of which are available through Altitude Publishing. Hendley lives in Toronto, Canada, with his girlfriend, Alyson, and two feisty cats. His website is located at www.natehendley.com.

ISBN 1-55265-102-9